FIRE YOUR BOSS

TRANSFORM YOUR LIFE FROM EMPLOYEE TO DIGITAL ENTREPRENEUR

HEMI HOSSAIN

FIRE YOUR BOSS

**TRANSFORM YOUR LIFE
FROM EMPLOYEE
TO DIGITAL
ENTREPRENEUR**

First published in 2020 by Dean Publishing
PO Box 119
Mt. Macedon, Victoria, 3441
Australia
deanpublishing.com

Copyright © Hemi Hossain

All rights reserved. No part of this publication may be reproduced, stored in a retrieval system or transmitted in any way or by any means, electronic, mechanical, photocopying, recording or otherwise, without the prior written permission of the publisher.

Cataloguing-in-Publication Data
National Library of Australia
Title: Fire Your Boss – Transform Your Life From Employee To Digital Entrepreneur
Edition: 2nd edn
ISBN: 978-1-925452-20-4
Category: BUSINESS/Entrepreneurship

The views and opinions expressed in this book are those of the author and do not necessarily reflect the official policy or position of any other agency, publisher, organization, employer or company. Assumptions made in the analysis are not reflective of the position of any entity other than the author(s) — and, these views are always subject to change, revision, and rethinking at any time.

The author, publisher or organizations are not to be held responsible for misuse, reuse, recycled and cited and/or uncited copies of content within this book by others.

*To my family, friends and
the people of Bangladesh.*

CONTENTS

One: Starting from Nothing 1

Two: The Day I Fired My Boss 13

Three: Let's Begin Your Business Transformation 23

Four: Working Smarter Not Harder 47

Five: Making Your Mind A Magnet For Success 55

How To Visualise 68

Six: My Entrepreneurship Journey 83

Seven: The Proximity Principle 103

Eight: Digital Dominance 109

Nine: Transform & Perform 121

The Program to Profit 151

About Hemi 155

Testimonials 157

End Notes 163

Book References 165

CHAPTER 1

STARTING FROM NOTHING

I was born in 1977, in a small village called Lalpur in Bangladesh, six years after Bangladesh became a sovereign and independent country. I was the fourth born of six siblings, the youngest son. Despite the heavy population in Bangladesh, I was lucky to grow up in a middle-class family, my father worked as a government employee and made a modest wage. He supported my mother and our family.

If I could use one word to describe growing up in Lalpur with my siblings, it would be "fun". We played together, always inventing new little games to entertain one another. We lived in a compact two-bedroom house, six of us kids in one room and mum and dad in the other. One of my younger sisters would often sneak into mum and dad's room at night to cosy up to them and give us a little more space.

Even though my father worked for the government, we were happily oblivious to the new government changes and political upheaval that swarmed Bangladesh at the time.

Growing up, I loved cricket. I had big dreams about being a professional cricket player and I played so often that I became really good. I liked to believe it was no coincidence that Bangladesh became an Associate member of the International Cricket Council the same year that I was born. I loved bowling, batting and fielding—and honed my all-rounder skills any opportunity I got.

The hours I spent playing cricket with my siblings and friends only fuelled by ambitions of becoming a professional cricket player. I could see myself wearing our National cricket uniform with our traditional colours of red and green. Unfortunately, my parents did not feel the same. They didn't allow such ambitious thinking and refused to support my love of the sport or buy me the equipment to play. They considered my cricket talents were nothing other than a hobby and they forbade me to pursue my dream of a career in cricket. To them, it was a waste of time. To me it was the ultimate dream.

Instead, I was pushed into study, even by my older siblings. I remember a time when I was physically pushed down at the desk by my older sister and forced to read. I felt helpless and discouraged. My dreams crushed. Instead, my family had their own dreams for me.

My father dreamt that I would one day become a doctor. He strongly suggested that I take up science in high school but I had no interest in this field whatsoever, and I grew disheartened. It seemed that my family were driven more by the prestigious lifestyle a career in medicine would bring than what my heart was telling me. I studied because I did not want to disappoint my father. However, I was not meant to work in the field of medicine and my grades reflected that. My father's disappointment in me was so strong that he refused to speak to me at all! In fact, it took an entire year before he would speak to me again.

I did what was expected of me through my teenage years. Though my heart often longed for a sporting career, I knew that would now never be. However, life suddenly changed for our family when I was 19 and all dreams were put on hold.

In 1996, my father retired from his government job and our family suffered not long thereafter. We stopped being a middle-class family and fell into poverty. Though we didn't live in a slum like many, we struggled for money to buy food and make ends meet. It was a frightening time for us. If we didn't do something, we could end up in a dire and unthinkable situation. I couldn't let that happen.

Something needed to change. As a nineteen-year-old man, I felt it was my duty to go out from the family home, find some work to help my family. I figured that I could get a job and send my family the money. But I was already dead broke. I didn't even know where to start.

I decided to move in with some friends in Dhaka, the capital city of Bangladesh and a few hours' drive from my family's home. Dhaka is a densely populated city, it is also the hub for job opportunities and commercial avenues in Bangladesh. I knew I had to try my luck, but with no money to my name, I wasn't at a great advantage. Luckily, my friends helped me as I was merely surviving.

I began to apply for many jobs. I went from job to job, still struggling to make ends meet and still struggling to send any money home. Waves of panic and guilt overcame me, I often thought of my family struggling back home and my desperation to help them grew each day. Hence, I decided to teach myself the ins-and-outs of putting computer parts together from scratch. I would pull them apart and study all their tiny electronic pieces, learning which part did what function. This seemed to create some opportunities for me. I was offered a job in a software development company to do some software programming for them. Though I was still just surviving, I felt it was a welcome break. Anything is better than poverty.

At this time, my older brother received a sponsorship to study and live in Canada. He was determined to use this opportunity to try to make money for the family too, although he also found it difficult.

I sent what little I could to my family but I knew it wasn't enough to sustain them.

A big thought dawned on me, maybe if I could somehow get overseas, I would come across some new unexplored opportunities to make more money for my family and myself. Then, one day, as if by chance, the opportunity arose. The company that I was working for was offered a contract to teach Microsoft Excel at the Australian High Commission. My company asked me to run the program. It was as if my dreams had been answered, only problem was I could not speak English and I didn't know anything about Australia. After some research about this far away country, I also found out that people living overseas could apply for international study at a university. I immediately applied. I had to try my luck.

Despite my concern about not speaking English, my boss was so confident in my ability to do this job that he called me aside one day and taught me some preliminary English-speaking protocols. He went through the basics of 'hello', 'nice to meet you', and other basic etiquette and explained that I could just point to the computer screen and teach it with minimal English.

During this time, he also taught me some Australian standards of courtesy: how to use utensils, how to speak, how to sit, how to engage with others. I took this very seriously. I studied body language and practiced every day.

Learning to eat with a knife, fork and spoon as an adult was a unique experience, and the feeling of putting metal in my mouth was rather odd at first. I studied all the new English protocols like I was studying for a PhD. I had this feeling inside, that my life depended on it, and my family's lives. I practised the hellos, thank yous, and common etiquette I had learned obsessively.

I finally got the chance to come to Australia with work but first had to pass a full day English test that included speaking, writing and listening. I thought that I had failed because I didn't really understand it. However, as coincidence would have it, not long after, a letter of offer came from an Australian university. They had accepted my university application and I was absolutely thrilled.

But one thing still lurked in the back of my mind—I had no money! My father could not support me and I asked everybody I knew to lend me some money so I could go to Australia. My uncle—who was quite well off—refused to help me. He just looked at me and said, "Forget about going overseas. Forget about this dream of yours. Just work!" I refused to listen to him and kept asking everyone I knew. Finally, one of my father's friends gave me some reprieve and lent me money to come to Australia. I felt so fortunate. Maybe my life could change now. Maybe I could find a way out for my family. Possibilities arose.

At this time, I was married and needed to leave my wife behind to start a life for us in Australia. This was a difficult decision but we knew it needed to be done. We needed to try something huge. We needed to be radical in our decisions in the hope that we could find a better life for ourselves and our families.

When I landed at Melbourne Airport, I called my contact here — my friend's sister. She told me to get a taxi because she couldn't come to pick me up. I had to get to a suburb called Laverton and had no idea about the direction to take or even if I was pronouncing the name of the suburb correctly.

My main concern was the lack of money I had to get me through. I had $600 only in my pocket and the taxi fare gobbled up $56 of it within my first hour of arriving. With the address in hand and a very nice taxi driver, I arrived at the house and was soon taken to another house where my sister's friend had organised for me to stay. It was a rental place in Footscray. This meant that I would be renting a room in a house with a stranger. I got to my 'new home' close to midnight with nothing but a small bag and a few hundred dollars. I didn't know what to do so I decided to sleep and see what the morning would bring.

In the morning, I finally met my new roommate. He was pleasant but straight to the point. He said, 'Rent is $270 per month and the bond is $270. I need it all upfront!'

This was basically everything I had. I negotiated that I would pay the rent now but the bond was unnecessary. I convinced him that I didn't have to pay the bond until I was more financially stable. Thankfully, he agreed.

Counting out my money, I now only had just over $300 left. $300 to get me through my new life. My life at Australia started with $300.

I made my way to the university all the while thinking I needed to get a job to survive. Any job! Quickly! I was told to ask around in Indian restaurants. I found a job as a kitchenhand after many hours of handing out my resume. I was offered $25 cash for a full day's work. I took it. The work was terrible. I hated every moment of it, but I kept thinking, 'I need to survive!' I was overqualified and underpaid. I cried myself to sleep every night. It was one of the most challenging times in my life. I felt I had no direction. I was lost. Lost in a foreign country with little money and lots of challenges. I was so focused on studying and saving money that I chose not to eat. I lived off steamed rice and lentils. I was starting to fade away. I went to university and studied during the day, then went to work all night. Surviving on little sleep and little food.

I was then offered a job at the franchise store 7-Eleven. I was told, I would have to do unpaid training for three months. By the end of the trial, I had lost roughly sixteen kilograms. and was only sleeping three to four hours per night. Finally, the boss decided to pay me, but it was only at $12 per hour. I was so desperate, I took it. I was just surviving, but still with nothing to show for it.

At this time, my wife was granted a visa and arrived in Australia. When I went to meet her at the airport, she did not recognise me. I had changed so drastically that I took her by surprise. I was thin, over-worked and hungry, but so happy to see her. Seeing her lifted my spirits.

I decided to apply for other jobs. I got a housekeeping job in a hotel. This was my first decent job where my employer followed Fair Works Wage Pay. For me, this was as good as it could get at that moment. I had already been in Australia for nine months by this time. The job required twenty hours of work per week. My wife and I both worked at the hotel doing housekeeping, and I also continued my studies. We began to see a change for the better financially and started to gain momentum. However, I was still worried about my tuition fees. Then my wife applied for a credit card and she got it. So I decided to pay my tuition fees with the credit card. I felt so rich. Everything was going so well. We decided to get our own place: we rented a two-bedroom apartment in Footscray.

Soon after, my studies began to suffer. I was still in survival mode. I didn't get the best marks in my third year. I went in to have a chat with the placement coordinator, Patrick as I had to go for an internship as part of my degree. He sat me down and told me that, my CV and interview had to be extraordinary if I were to have a chance at an internship and a well-paid job. I got an internship in the computer industry as a junior programmer but I was working for free.

I was working at the Crown Casino at night and working at the internship during the day. Each night I would go home after work and improve my communication skills in front of the mirror. I would practice my body language and stay up as late as I could, reciting interviews in my mind. I had no money to buy a computer so I decided to create my own. I obtained old computer parts and built a computer from scratch. To me, having a computer symbolised an image of wealth and prosperity through corporate success. I wanted that. I would watch people in suits on the train and dream that one day I would be just like them. I was seeing myself, in my mind, as that successful man, going to work on a train while reading a book, on my way to my successful job. This was part of my job: to envision it. To see it in my mind's eye.

Every night for three months I practiced and I visualised relentlessly. I then decided to apply for other jobs. With Patrick's help, I got an internship as a programmer. He was one of my greatest teachers and I am so grateful to him.

I had so many financial debts at this time that I felt I needed to get ahead. The credit card debt accumulated and the stress was getting to me. I only slept a couple of hours every night and worked the rest of the time. I took my internship and my work very seriously. I knew all this valuable experience would help me reach my goal of success.

Throughout this whole period, my wife was my support. My backbone. She allowed me to do what I felt I needed to do to get us to the point where we were free from poverty and living a life of prosperity. She, too, worked alongside me, assisting in our endeavour to make a better life for ourselves. We were a team and we still are. She has always believed in me and I am so grateful to her. I always found that no matter how bad things got, I was grateful for the opportunities opening up for me. As my wife and I worked so much, there was little time for anything else. No leisure activities or hanging out with friends. It was all work and no play. This also happened to be my undoing!

After one year of working at my internship as a programmer, I got offered a permanent part-time role. I desperately needed full-time work with steady pay. I decided to not take the part-time offer after the internship and look for something full-time. I applied for a few jobs and got them but decided to take a role at the ANZ bank. I worked for a great manager, and for the first time, someone saw my potential to be more! She offered me more than guidance, she allowed me to be who I am, seeing the leader within me and encouraging me to take on more work responsibilities. I was now earning a great wage and loving my job. For the first time in my life, I felt things were beginning to look up.

Everything was going smoothly. My wife and I were both working. Financially, I found that we were finally making more than ends meet. Then, one day, out-of-the-blue—I felt quite unwell. I was in so much pain that I had to go to hospital. The pain brought me to tears. I was doubled over in pain. The doctors ordered tests. They couldn't find the cause, so they sent me home. I decided that it was just a stomach bug and went back to work. A few nights later, I ended up in the emergency room again. This time the pain was more severe and they assigned a specialist to my case.

During this time I experienced significant weight loss and after many tests, I was diagnosed with a severe case of pancreatitis. Pancreatitis is inflammation of the pancreas that occurs when enzymes start to attack the pancreas itself. It commonly affects people who drink alcohol, which for me was very strange, as I wasn't drinking.

After some discussions with the doctor, he put it down to chronic stress. I was advised not to physically work as some severe pancreatitis can result in organ failure and even death. My wife had to work during the day and sit with me all night. We were back to square one. No money! I was advised by my doctor to go on Centrelink benefits. My boss refused and told me she would pay me sick leave as long as I needed it. I was so grateful.

During this time in my life, I began to question everything I had done up until this point. What was the point of it all? To make money? My prognosis was grim. I was still in a bad condition. The chronic pain left me with only two options: to have surgery to try to rectify the situation and possibly die, or wait and see and possibly die waiting. My options weren't great.

I questioned life even more. I began to wonder: What is the difference between me and someone else who does nothing? What will I leave behind when I go? No one will remember me tomorrow. What's the meaning behind all this struggle?

Something had to change.

I had to change.

This is when I decided, if I survived, I must leave a legacy. That I would do something worthwhile. I would make a difference. I wanted change and it needed to start with me.

I decided I wanted two things:
- Financial freedom.
- To help others.

This is what I chose for myself if I survived—and I was damn sure not going to let anyone stop me!

"If you just work on stuff that you like and you're passionate about, you don't have to have a master plan with how things will play out."
— **Mark Zuckerberg, *Facebook Founder and CEO***

CHAPTER 2

THE DAY I FIRED MY BOSS

While I was in hospital, my wife and I discussed the options available to me. She wanted me to have surgery as she believed it was the only way I would survive. However, before I could make a decision, the surgeon wanted to discuss some things with me.

He questioned me about my life, my lifestyle and everything happening at the time. He suggested that the pain and diagnosis was most likely from my lifestyle and the pressure I have put on myself through my work. He advised me to wait it out. He asked me to postpone the surgery and wait a week. I asked him if it was too risky to wait. He said, "Let's see how it goes", which I took as "If you die, you die."

That was the longest week of my entire life. Each day,

when I woke, I felt I was counting down the days to my death. I was petrified of dying. I couldn't walk and was bedridden. I was only drinking water as food was making me feel worse. This was the period in my life where I could really reflect. After all, I had no choice. I could wait to die or reflect and change my thinking.

As I was in bed, sick and weak—suddenly it felt like a light bulb went off in my mind; I realised that I should be working for myself. I wanted financial freedom and the freedom of more time—and that could only happen if I was my own boss. Currently, the company paid for my skills and work hours, but I realised that I could use those same hours for myself and perhaps earn more. If I used my time wisely, I could earn more money and have more freedom. No job other than working for myself could give me this same level of freedom. Now, all I needed to do with this newfound inspiration was get well and make it happen.

Day seven arrived and I was petrified. Thoughts raced around in my mind. I was not ready to die. The doctor could see I was getting better so he asked me to wait more. To hold off the surgery. Then day eight, nine, ten. For the first time in my life, I had ample time to think and reflect.

Twenty days later, I got better. I went in to see the surgeon for our scheduled appointment. I felt so much stronger, much more driven and much healthier. It felt like a miracle that I was walking. Coming from death's door, here I was, having tests that came up negative and clear. I was relaxed, eating healthy and sleeping more. I realised that I like feeling strong.

I knew this was a wake-up call. I was lucky. Death didn't arrive. This is when I decided to quit my job at the bank. My manager didn't want to let me go, but she knew that I had to pursue my dream. She knew that I was worth so much more and had the potential to do great things. She hesitantly supported me and let me go—but I had already decided that I needed to be my own boss and nobody could change my mind.

I decided I would start my own business. What business, though? I had no idea what I wanted to do. I thought about it for a couple of months and realised that I needed a steady wage while I decided. So, again, I applied for a job with City West Water and got it. I worked there for eleven months. I was cruising through it, as it was a nine-to-five job with no overtime. I actually had a life outside of work!

The money was good and I was slowly but surely feeling stronger and healthier with each passing day. I ate well, took care of myself, went to bed early and made small changes to take care of myself. I was too scared to end up six-foot under with no legacy to leave behind.

Having my own business still lingered heavily in the back of my mind.

Then I did something really stupid. I followed what everyone else was doing. I went and bought a house. I put us into more debt because I thought—at the time—that that was what was expected of me. I fell back into an old thinking pattern. I felt the social pressure and succumbed to it.

Around the same time, I realised that I wasn't really enjoying my job so I decided to quit. I took on another role in Springvale (thinking it would be a more prestigious place to work) as a Business Lead Analyst in MYOB. I drove for hours every day in traffic to get to work. This only lasted six months before I took on a role at Telstra as a Business Manager. This is where my wage shot up. I now had a team that I was in charge of—but my heart was not totally in it—my dream to be my own boss kept nagging at me. At Telstra, I had the best boss and mentor. She saw the natural leadership skills in me. She encouraged me to go further. She supported every move I made. I began to think about what she used to tell me; her words of encouragement circled round in my mind. Little did she know the whirlwind of positivity was fuelling my passion even more.

So one day, I googled 'natural leadership' and found a website that mentioned 'life coaching'. I immediately enrolled in a life coaching course and found that it was what I had been looking for. I found my calling. I learned so much about myself during this time. By 2010, Telstra had put me into a leadership program and I was at the top of my game. I had come across challenges and defeated them every single time, learning more and more about myself.

During this time, my wife and I also began to talk about starting our family. We were in a good position and had been married for ten years already. We were so career-focused that we had never stopped to think about having a family—until this point.

After trying to conceive for almost a year, we didn't have much luck. We went to the doctor again to make sure everything was all right. He asked us both to change our lifestyles and eat healthier. This surprised us and we began to understand the value of a healthy lifestyle. We decided to get healthier. A year later, in 2012, our first child, a boy, was born. My career was progressing at Telstra and we were building our dream home. I felt happy and successful. Life was awesome.

I really thought that I was finally free. I was in a good job and making good money. But this was a dream world, a fantasy land. With a house mortgage, a child, learning courses and living expenses—our debt was increasing and I was frustrated. I wasn't entirely sure what was wrong!

I started reflecting a lot again and decided that life coaching would be my business. I brainstormed all the possibilities to identify my niche. Until one day, I realised how many people were in the same situation as when I first came to Australia. These immigrants would all need my help. To make their lives easier, I could teach them what I did to start a new life in a foreign country. To find work and build success.

I developed a 6-week program: Career Coaching. I would talk to clients on the phone, via Skype and would teach them everything I had learned. I would teach them courtesy and language and how to behave in interviews. I would help them get jobs. My business grew and I had less and less time. So, in order to continue my life coaching work, I once again decided I needed to quit my day job.

I was certain this time—but I definitely needed a steady source of income. I wanted to take the risk but my boss did not want me to leave. She knew my potential but also loved me in my role. I wanted time with my family and financial freedom, so I decided to stay. I worked so hard and with all the over-time the stress began to build again. I knew that I could not keep this up.

My son was four years old and my wife was pregnant again. It wasn't entirely wise at the time to leave a steady income and pursue my passion. But I was determined and confident this time and had to listen to my heart.

My signature workshop 'Leadership with Influence' was born. I went to different companies and ran workshops for them on the weekends. During this time I saw an opportunity to go back to Bangladesh and teach people before they came to Australia. I engaged my contacts in Bangladesh to run the workshop for my fellow countrymen and I started to get more and more work overseas.

This was the day that I realised that I had fired my boss, and that life for me was just beginning.

BUILD YOUR ROCK-SOLID FOUNDATION FOR SUCCESS

Before, we go any further into my story, I am going to take this moment to ask you to STOP. You need to understand that you have to build a foundation before you set off on your journey. Before you go and just randomly fire your boss.

Sure, you can set off on your adventure, much like I did, without a foundation and with the sole focus of making money. However, that's like setting off to hike in the wilderness without a map to guide you—it can make you go around and around in circles instead of heading in the right direction. Believe me, it's a thousand times easier with a map pointing the right way for you.

And that's what this book is about. It's a guide-map. It's a support to give you a way through. That's why I have written this book. So you can avoid half the obstacles I ran into. You can have an easier path to your journey of success.

You see, you don't have to figure out everything yourself. Humanity is built on learning and growing from the past and other people so we can build a new and better future.

Remember: the more ambitious your goals are, the stronger the foundations you'll need to build.

So, if you prefer to have a tried-and-tested map that shows you the way, rather than trying to figure it all out yourself, please take the time to read this book and answer all the questions along the way. This book is essentially for you.

If you read this book and do the exercises I have outlined. It will help you to:

- » Build a moving-forward mindset programmed for success
- » Build a foundation for success
- » Develop new insights about your strengths and help them grow
- » Give you strategies to build a successful life and career
- » Help you avoid a lot of the traps and pitfalls many people fall into
- » Give you new-found confidence to further your career
- » Show you unique ways to fire your boss and live the life of your dreams.

You see, I did it from nothing and that means you can too! This book is delivered to you in two parts:

1. My journey
2. Your journey

You see, we are actually taking this journey together. I will share with you all my struggles and battles. I will share all my vulnerabilities and challenges so you can learn from them.

As Eleanor Roosevelt said, "Learn from the mistakes of others. You can't live long enough to make them all yourself."

But I won't just offer you the hard times, I will also give you real strategies to help you transform yourself and live a life of greater freedom.

Because in the long run, everybody wants a life of freedom. A life that is a result of your own personal choices. It's empowering to create your own life. It's exciting to move forward and gain more momentum.

This book is designed to get you to the other side—to the side of success. To the side of choice and freedom. And to do this I am offering you a strategic step-by-step plan. A plan to take you from employee to entrepreneur. To move you out of a victim mindset and into a leadership mindset.

Now, it doesn't matter how long this journey takes. Learning and growing is a life-long journey. It took me years to find the courage and develop the skills to become an entrepreneur—but as I said, time isn't the main issue. The main thing that matters is that you are moving forward, that you are developing and growing from where you currently are.

There is always more knowledge to gain and wisdom to develop—but we only gain that when we venture beyond our comfort zone and stretch ourselves a little further.

> *"Life always begins with one step outside of your comfort zone."*
> *— Shannon L. Alder*

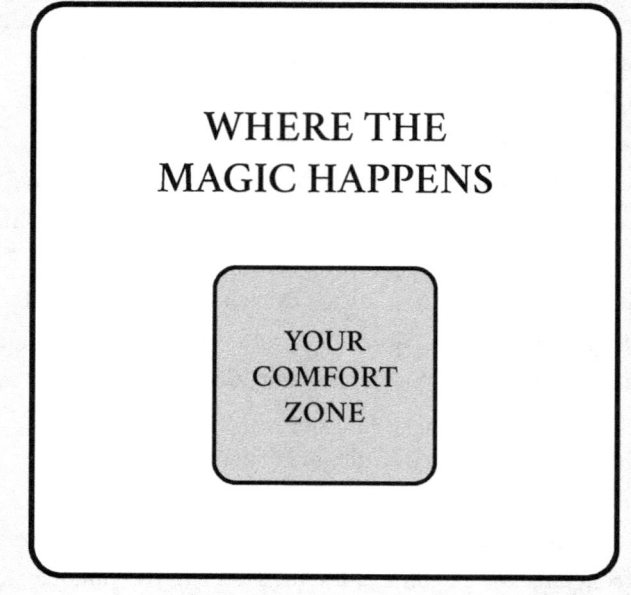

I am going to offer you a 7-step path to success. The 7 essential steps you'll need to move in the directions of your dreams. The 7 steps that I used to transform from employee to digital entrepreneur.

And furthermore, the last step gives you a step-by-step process that you can follow to continue in the direction of your dreams and never look back!

I am going to give you ALL of them in this book and I will walk you through each step. I will share my journey and simultaneously focus on yours. Yes, we will take this journey of success together.

> *"You shouldn't focus on why you can't do something, which is what most people do. You should focus on why perhaps you can, and be one of the exceptions."*
> — **Steve Case, AOL Co-Founder and CEO**

CHAPTER 3

LET'S BEGIN YOUR BUSINESS TRANSFORMATION

When you think of some of the global businesses that have seen rapid growth in the past decade, many are following disruptive models. They are changing the old system of business and breaking new ground. Think of Netflix, Uber, Airbnb, Amazon Prime.

The thinkers behind these organisations are a new generation of forward-thinking, rule-breaking entrepreneurs who don't care about the way things have always been done, instead they focus on growth and innovation. They streamlined processes and embraced technological innovations to ensure they could easily adapt to any industry changes. Yes, of course they are world-class companies and have the ability to do things that many small businesses can't, but that's not the point.

The point is—you can have your own transformation.

You see, a business transformation is essentially a term for making fundamental changes in how a business runs. This includes staff, processes, systems and technology. These transformations help businesses compete more effectively, become more efficient, and usually drives their profits up too.

Now, a "business transformation"—isn't all about processes, growth and technological changes—it's really a mindset change and restructure in the way they have been doing business. In many ways, it's a way to create more impact and embrace new possibilities through change.

Now, what if you could go through the same type of transformation? That you could look at new ways to change and grow. New ideas you can incorporate in order to make your biggest dreams become a reality.

Here is the journey that I have taken, and the path I have shown many others who want to move forward in their career and their lives.

I have put them in order for you and given you specific questions and activities to lead you in the direction of success.

If you follow this path I can guarantee that you will have more time, more freedom, more money and more happiness.

Are you ready to transform?

7 ESSENTIAL STEPS TO TRANSFORM FROM EMPLOYEE TO DIGITAL ENTREPRENEUR

1. Build your Foundations for Success
2. Assess Yourself for Success
3. Cultivate a Moving-Forward Mindset
4. Maximise Your Time and Worth
5. Use the Proximity Principle

6. Use the Power of Digital Marketing
7. Transform and Perform — Use The 9P Business Strategy

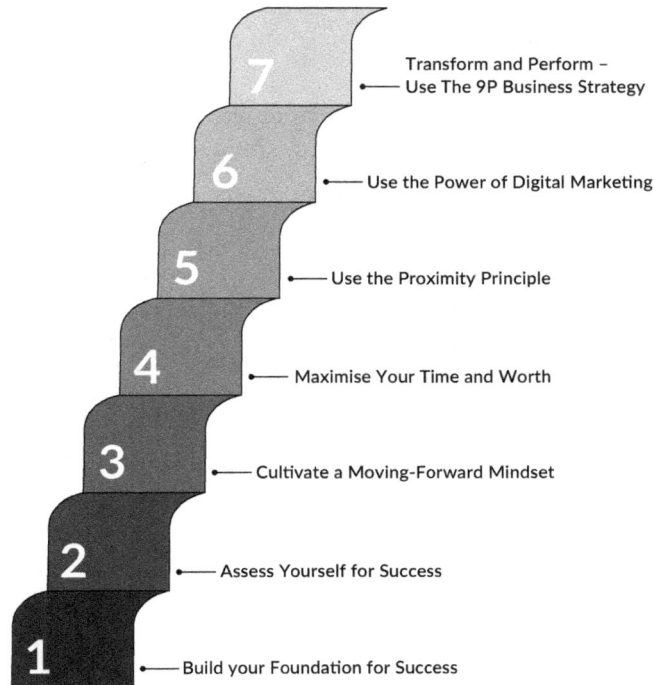

STEP 1: BUILD YOUR FOUNDATION FOR SUCCESS

Any builder or architect knows that a solid foundation is essential for any building to survive storms and bad weather. The foundation needs to be rock-solid so the building structure is well supported.

This is the same principle for us.

We need firm foundations before we build the new structure of our life.

Now, here's something you need to know. Even if you're at rock-bottom—you can build from there.

In fact, the famous writer of the Harry Potter series, J.K Rowling said, "Rock bottom became the solid foundation in, which I built my life."

I can assure you, I also built my foundations from rock bottom.

The foundations are your inner set of principles. Your dreams and goals. Your vision of the future.

I discovered my foundations from personal reflection. From asking myself some deep and honest questions. It's important to get real. To ask yourself some soul-searching questions and answer them honestly. Let's begin.

The Freedom Questions
- What does freedom look like to you? Write down your vision of what it means for you to be free. What does your free life look like?

- What do you want to be free from?

- What areas you are currently not free from?

The Dream Questions
- What do you dream about? Do you dream about the career that your parents wanted for you? Or do you have some inner dreams of your own?

- Are you fighting against what others see you as doing or being?

- Are you currently living the life of your dreams? If not, what is holding you back?

- Consider now what your ideal life looks like. Write it down clearly and in detail.

- If you could do anything in the world, what would it be?

This is where you need to get real with yourself and begin to see that you can make this dream happen, regardless of the circumstances surrounding you, or even the circumstances of your past. Let yourself dream. Be bold in your dreaming.

Know Your Values

Values are the principles that help us give life meaning. They are what we honour and give value to. Values also help us to persevere through adversity.

Our values and beliefs drive our life. We all need to find out what is driving us and where that came from.

You may value things like: family, authenticity, honesty, fun, kindness, dependability, courage, reliability.

- Make a list of your core values. Things that you value regardless of the circumstances in your life.

- Focus on giving and adding values to other's lives too. Make a list of where and how you can and do add value to other people.

Review Your Education Options
- Education

It is never too late to learn more. If you find yourself dreaming of a better life, look at ways you can begin to make that happen. Education is important, as is self-motivation and determination. Set your goals and go steady. Short courses and personal development will always enrich your life in more ways than you can count. Do not be afraid to get educated. Education can be acquired from anywhere. Even online. Do your research on what is relevant and appropriate for you. You can even learn from YouTube. Learn!

- What new skill or piece of information can you learn that will help you move closer to your dream life? Perhaps it's to improve your speaking and communication skills, maybe it's to study a course or get a diploma.

- What knowledge do you need most to move yourself and your career forward?

Develop a Positive Mindset

Keeping on track with goals can often become overwhelming and frustrating. One key aspect here is to stay positive and keep your head up. Do not allow your past, your family or anyone else influence you into thinking that you are not good enough or not worthy enough. You are the only one who can change it for yourself, so keep going and focus on your goals.

Ask yourself these simple questions:
- What can you say to yourself in order to remain positive?

- Who is a positive support in your life?

  ....

  ....

  ....

  ....

- What positive thoughts can you have to help you stay focused and keep going?

  ....

  ....

  ....

  ....

  ....

A list of affirmations that can be helpful:
- I believe in me.
- I can achieve anything I put my mind to.
- The world wants more of what I have to offer.
- There is nobody else in the world like me. That is my magic.
- I believe in my abilities.
- I will always find a way to reach my goals.
- I am a magnet for success.
- I know my worth. I am worthy of a great income.
- I am able to overcome obstacles with ease.
- I have many skills and strengths.
- I have the inner strength to navigate any and all challenges.
- I am successful and take pride in the work I do.
- When I work, I apply myself with focus and positivity.

The Secret I Was Taught by a College Teacher

One day, when I was very frustrated, I went to a college teacher and confided in him about my struggles. He told me something that I have never forgotten and have used throughout my ups and downs. He said, "Life is boring if you don't have challenges and struggles. You must take every challenge as an opportunity."

I still remember his advice and it's helped me a lot throughout life. I have followed his advice and tried to turn every challenge into an opportunity to learn, grow and discover. To see life as an adventure.

I also noticed that life is all about discipline and creating habits that work for you. The difference between successful and unsuccessful people is their habits and discipline. Without discipline, I could not have completed my internship, forged ahead in my life or become a successful entrepreneur.

Jim Rohn once said, "Motivation is what gets you started. Habit is what keeps you going". He also said, "Discipline is the bridge between goals and accomplishment".

Let's say that again—*discipline is the bridge between goals and accomplishments.*

Yes, if you want to get to the other side, if you want your goals to actually come to fruition—you must walk the bridge of discipline. Laziness will make the bridge collapse and leave you stranded on the poor side of town. Discipline is what you use when you don't feel like doing something.

I can tell you, there have been thousands of times when I didn't want to get up for work, I wanted to press that snooze button and roll over into my comfortable bed. There have been many times I nearly listened to that voice in my head telling me, "It's too hard. It's too far. It's out of reach." You have to develop the discipline of believing in yourself.

The habit of making your dreams a priority. Laziness and half-baked goals won't get you anywhere, they'll only get you frustrated and upset.

How do you think Muhammad Ali became a boxing sensation? He trained. He didn't like it but he did it. He said, *"I hated every minute of training, but I said, 'Don't quit. Suffer now and live the rest of your life as a champion."*

Yes, this is what discipline and habits can do. They make you live the rest of your life as a champion. Sure, that doesn't mean as the heavy weight champion of the world necessarily, but as the champion of your life, pursuing your dreams, on your terms.

A study published in the *Journal of Personality*[1] showed a strong correlation between people with high levels of self-discipline and their overall satisfaction in life. In fact, disciplined people enjoyed their success and gained it more often because their lives were structured for long-term gain. It also showed that discipline can help manage your day-to-day stress and can improve your health. (Unless you went overboard like me and then it wrecks your health).

But having a process you can use to become more disciplined and focus your efforts gives you the power to make progress and achieve your dreams. However, in doing this, remember that your health is more important than anything. A healthy lifestyle makes you a success magnet! Too much stress and overworking can cause health issues so it's important to keep a healthy balance.

---

1. *Journal of Personality*, 2014, Yes, but are they happy? Effects of trait self-control on affective well-being and life satisfaction. Hofmann W(1), Luhmann M, Fisher RR, Vohs KD, Baumeister RF. University of Chicago.. Epub 2013 Aug 8.

STEP 2: ASSESS YOURSELF FOR SUCCESS

Part of any success is to assess deeper questions about your situation. Once you have built a good foundation, it's important to assess your current situation. This way you can get a bird's-eye view on what you want to change and what you don't.

You can't improve what you don't assess. It's not always easy to take stock and take a good honest look at where you are in life—but without doing that you can never move forward.

> *"Mentally make an effort to assess every step you're taking in all aspects of your life – including in your career, your relationships, and your health – in terms of directionality. That is, ask yourself, in which way am I truly moving? Am I getting away from my originating place, or am I returning to it?"*
> **— Dr Wayne W. Dyer**

YOUR CAREER PATH

Now, because this book is focused on your career more than any other part—I'm going to focus on that right now, however, you can use this process for other parts of your life too. Let's delve deeper.

Assess Where You Are Right Now
- Do you like your current situation?

....

....

....

- Are you in your current job by choice or by default?

- Are you fulfilling a promise you made as a child to your family?

- Whose life are you currently living? The one expected of you or the one you chose?

Take some time to assess how you got into your current situation. Try to avoid placing blame on anyone or anything Take a good, hard look at what brought you to this point.

Recognise that, once you discover who you truly are, your inner self will now allow you to do anything. This is where you may feel the struggle, as I did, for all those years. Take the time to reinvent yourself or to find what your true passion is—without judgement or fear. You have full permission to explore this.

Assess What's Not Working?

- Are you dissatisfied with your job? Why?
  Answer this question honestly and write it out so you can understand what aspects of your job you are dissatisfied with and why.

....
....
....
....
....
....
....
....

- What areas of your career aren't working and why?

....
....
....
....
....
....
....
....
....
....
....

Assess What is Working?

- What is currently working well in your life?

  ....
  ....
  ....
  ....
  ....
  ....
  ....
  ....

- What is currently working in your career? Are there moments of fulfilment, meaning, or joy in your work?

  ....
  ....
  ....
  ....
  ....
  ....
  ....
  ....
  ....
  ....
  ....
  ....
  ....
  ....
  ....

- Can you list any great moments in your current job, or do you need to seek a new job that would provide more of those experiences?

- If inspiration with your current work is fading, ask yourself if you have outgrown this work. Do you need to move on?

- What do you need to do to get that inspiration back?

Assess Where You Are Stuck?

At work, there can be a lot to deal with, such as never-ending to-do lists, new responsibilities, pointless meetings, toxic co-workers, office politics, impossible deadlines, lack of leadership, poor career prospects and biased bosses. These numerous demands can all lead to exhaustion, disengagement, lack of passion and burnout. And you can invent a myriad of reasons and justifications for remaining stuck—some reasons can be completely valid and some merely excuses.

You may feel suffocated at your work place; it is filled with files and paper and money but no heart? Does it lack human-to-human connection?

Do you feel like a robot assigned to do task after task with no clear purpose?

This is where you choose, where you decide what you want.

Make a small list of some positive changes you can make to make your work life feel better.

Then get rid of anything that does not align with your

....

....

....

....

....

....

....

....

....

....

vision. This may mean that you will have to get out and start looking for other work to get an understanding of who you really are and what you are capable of.

Assess Why You're Stuck

The money: If you feel like you can't leave the job because it's only there as a means to an end, then you are choosing to remain in a position that makes you feel uncomfortable and unhappy. For example, if you took a new job role simply because of the money, but now your career is all-encompassing and you don't have any work-life balance.

At certain ages and certain stages, your career is number one. But as you're building your future, you'll start looking toward your overall life goals: How does the job or career that you've selected fit into all the other things you want in life?

Becoming too comfortable in the job: You have been doing the same kind of work for years now, and you feel too comfortable because now you can do it effortlessly. You stay as far away as possible from change and accepting something new that's coming your way without realising the monotony it is ultimately creating in your life, leaving you with no chance of advancement in your career or personal growth. Quitting a job or seeking a new career can create the greatest amount of discomfort in your life. The discomfort of the departure from what you know in life is what will allow you to change it for the better. It is important to remember that comfort can lead to complacency, whereas discomfort can allow you to grow.

Your job title has become your status symbol: Most people value their career successes. I do too. It's great to be proud of what you do. But it becomes a trap when you wear your job title like a badge of worth and make in incongruent with who you are. A professional identity that you are proud of is wonderful but if it becomes an avenue for boost your ego or self-importance, then you need to take a look at yourself.

You may hold a reputable position in your company, which satisfies your egoistic needs. However, this may also be draining all your time and energy into work you may not completely enjoy. You choose to stick with it because your ego does not allow you to give up and be portrayed as a loser or unsuccessful. It becomes the status quo to be miserable—with a prestigious title.

If this sounds familiar, it's time for you to get some perspective. Consider what matters to you outside of your career. What are your special talents? What are your hobbies? What causes or charities do you care about? Your self-worth will be compromised if you only focus on your career.

Getting out of touch with your values and drivers: Many people will betray their primary values for work. This can become a very big mistake. Do not allow yourself to get out of touch with who you are and the values you hold.

People are chasing money and losing work–life balance. Though it seems that money is the primary driver for a person to pursue a job, there are other drivers, and without their fulfilment one can never be satisfied.

These drivers can be:
- Autonomy: having freedom.
- Creativity: trying new things and exploring new

options.

- Competition: a career value based on competing with others rather than trying to be the best version of yourself.
- Management: moving up in career progression.

When you finally acknowledge your worth, you can then begin to create the life you want and make the difficult decisions to make it happen.

> *"Everyone has been made for some particular work, and the desire for that work has been put in every heart."*
> — ***Rumi***

Hemi is sharing more in his INTERACTIVE book.

See exclusive, behind-the-scenes videos, audios and photos.

DOWNLOAD free content and learn how to Grow With Hemi.

growwithhemi.com/interactive

HEMI'S TOP TIPS

FOR SAILING ABOVE THE MIDDLE CLASS

- **Know your driving force.**
  You have to be motivated enough to work for the cause you believe in; otherwise, anything you do will seem boring and burdensome. You won't be motivated to do it. This will leave you back where you started, only more frustrated.

- **Learn to be stubborn.**
  Don't let anybody influence you in the way they feel is best for you. Go the way you feel you need to go.

- **Be persistent.**
  Don't let failure get in the way. Learn from it.

- **See yourself as a winner.**
  You must visualise yourself as you wish to be every single day. Make it a power habit.

- **Take risks.**
  Take calculated risks when you need to.
  "Man cannot discover new oceans unless he has the courage to lose sight of the shore."
  — André Gide

- **Have courage.**
  Don't be scared to try new tricks and strategies.

- **Seize opportunity.**
  Don't let financial risk stop you from taking an advantageous opportunity.

- **Invest in yourself.**
  Put your money towards mental development and skill development because you are your greatest asset.

- **Read obsessively.**
  Readers are leaders. Buy some great books and make sure to read them every day. Something you read can give you a new idea or a new tactic—or it can simply keep you motivated.

- **Be willing to relocate.**
  Sometimes opportunity doesn't knock on your door. Sometimes you have to go hunt for it. Sometimes you have to go and knock the door down yourself. Don't hesitate to move out of your city or even out of the country if there is a better opportunity waiting there.

- **Take financial responsibility.**
  Financial instability is the natural and predictable result of ongoing poor choices. Until you realise this and start taking responsibility for your own financial situation, you will not be wealthy and successful.

- **Don't be just satisfied.**
  'Constant dissatisfaction' sounds negative, but it's actually very positive because it keeps you aiming high and working for more and more.

CHAPTER 4

WORKING SMARTER NOT HARDER

When I was working full-time, working overtime, and putting all my energy into 'climbing the ladder', I found that I was chasing one dream and one dream only: *to get rich!*

Slowly, my hard work began to pay off and I got a promotion, which led me to work harder for the next promotion. I kept piling on the workload and spent more of my time in the office, working harder every day to get to the top. I got there. I made it to the top! But it came at a big price.

At the top, I was supposed to be happy, rich, financially stable and with enough free time, right? Instead, I found myself in more debt. I became very anxious and suffered from anxiety attacks, falling very ill again in 2012. This wasn't part of the plan.

I realised that all my over-time and hard work was only benefitting the company I worked for. My lifestyle was a complete mess. I had no down time or family time. I had compromised my goals and integrity in order to get ahead.

Many people can relate to my story.

Many people believe you must work hard to get rich and work yourself to the bone in order to stay ahead. This is where these misconceptions begin. This is only half the story. It is not enough to just work hard to make money and set some aside for a rainy day. To ensure your future wealth, you must work equally smart.

Hard work has little to do with success. Studies have shown that the reason why this strategy of hard work doesn't pay off is because, after fifty hours of productive time, your productivity goes down. Furthermore, if you continue to push yourself, often due to lack of sleep and self-care, you will also encounter failed relationships, failed social connections and a drop off in performance. Too much hard work slows down your growth. Working hard initially is not a bad idea but with time you need to learn how to accomplish more with less work.

Wanting to be rich is a fantastic goal but working yourself to the bone is not the answer. You must embrace risk and be willing to be uncomfortable if you want to be rich and successful. This can mean detaching from the stability of a regular job. To transform yourself from employee to entrepreneur.

There is a limit to what you can earn in a job. You might climb the managerial ladder and progress a little but, once you get more, it makes you want even more. You run the risk of becoming materialistic, focusing solely on the money. More disposable income means more spending, which leads to more things, and more debt. However, unless you find a way to convert $100,000 into $1,000,000, you are still stuck in that 'middle-class' mindset. Being rich will always be too far away. Working smarter is the only way forward.

Now, I know this may be a new idea to some people. We have been conditioned to believe that hard work is the only way. And though I believe in the power of hustling and creating massive opportunities with working hard, we eventually arrive at the conclusion that working harder does not guarantee us more money.

Let me explain.

Here's why:

1. You Become Too Attached to Comfort

When people have a secure job they begin to feel safe and comfortable. They save a little as they go along in their comfortable world. Now, there's nothing wrong with comfort and security but all too often people become complacent and decide to choose comfort over growth. When you're on cruise-control in life, why would you touch the accelerator right? A secure job and life can be great for a while but if you decide never to take risks or push yourself out of your comfort zone then you're choosing comfort as your primary objective. If you lost your job tomorrow, how would your life change? Would it kick-start you into a choice to follow your dream, or would you just look for another job?

You can choose to shake things up a little. Right now, you can choose to make one small change and take charge of your future.

Working in a job does not really allow or encourage you to take risks. You are exchanging your time for money. When you're trading time for money, your income will always be limited.

This creates a repetitive cycle and your own personal 'comfort zone'. There is no room here to create additional income-producing activities.

You need to take risks to create wealth in life. Entrepreneurs are always willing to take big risks and lay things on the line to be successful.

2. Time is More Valuable Than Money

The incredible thing about money is that you can always make more of it. Unfortunately, we can't say the same for time. No human on earth has the magical ability to produce more time than the other. When you spend time, that's it! When you spend money, you can always get more. When you work for a boss you don't get the chance to use that valuable time for yourself. You use it for them in order to grow their business. Sure, you get paid but you are using your most valuable commodity (time) on their dreams and goals and not your own. If you're on a salary or contract arrangement, you may be working over-time too — that's time you're not getting back! When you work for yourself, you may in fact have to work harder than when you work for someone else, but you're in control of how to spend your time. You are using time to benefit you and your future.

Most jobs these days are a trade-off. You are trading your time for money. You are given a certain amount of money in order to work a certain amount of time. This simple equation of exchanging time for money has a limit. You eventually hit a roadblock! Why? Because you only have a certain amount of time in each day and each week, which means that you' earning potential is limited. That's the system when you exchange time for money. Time is the most valuable commodity out there. If you are constantly trading your time for money, then being wealthy may be a goal that is never achieved. There are only 24 hours in a day. Your choice now is to use them wisely.

3. You Stop Learning

Working within the constraints of a nine-to-five job can hinder self-education and learning due to the workload. By the time you finish your work day, you are probably too exhausted to even think about doing anything other than sleep.

As an entrepreneur, I find that I put aside a great deal of time for self-improvement through learning. I take the time to learn more so that I can teach more and therefore create more opportunities to make more money. Capitalising on self-education is crucial. However, when I was working those long hours, I found it difficult to stay on task with my learning. There are just not enough hours in the day to do both.

Rich people understand that true wealth is not measured in terms of an annual salary or wages but in net worth and deeper ways that can't be measured like freedom and time. It is a completely different way of thinking about your personal earnings. And they continue to grow rich because of this mindset.

Being rich isn't just about money. True wealth is about doing what you love while creating time and financial freedom.

4. You Think Saving is the Saviour

Saving money is an awesome thing to do. Who doesn't want a handsome sum of money nestled comfortably in their bank account? But you need to understand the huge difference between saving money and making money. You may be able to save fifty dollars on changing your electricity supplier, but your electricity supplier isn't making you money. You may save a few dollars by skipping that additional muffin with your morning coffee but that muffin isn't producing money for you. Let me repeat: saving money and making money are not the same thing.

Both are good but you need to know the difference first. Making more money means you can save more money. Investing your money is smarter than simply trying to hoard small leftovers from your weekly pay packet. Investing in your business can help you make money and save money all at the same time. Investing the money that you make on other things that also grow your money is even better. You may have heard the quote, "money doesn't grow on trees" and it doesn't, but money can grow in business. Businesses are designed to be mega money plantations that grow stronger each year.

This doesn't mean that money will simply jump into your pocket, you have to make it work for you first. You have to be dedicated to making your money grow. Entrepreneurs are usually great at this. They can see the potential to make money and are driven to understand that money can be saved, grown, invested and compounded. They educate themselves in a whole manner of ways, always looking for the edge. Employees on the other hand often focus on chipping away and using any leftovers to save in a bank account. Employees are usually more worried about losing their 'cash cow' (their boss) whereas entrepreneurs know they are the boss and the cash cow. They make money work for them like an employee.

Investing is one way to make money your employee. You see, the entire role of an employee is to make money for the boss right? Well, money can do this too. Money is the ultimate employee—it can make more money for you, without you having to pay for its holiday or sick pay. It doesn't complain or ask for benefits either. It simply grows if you know how to invest it right.

5. You're Making Someone Else Rich

When you're an employee your role is made in order to make your boss rich. This is fine if you're happy with that arrangement. You work for them and you help them make more money. They give you a limited supply of that money in order to feel safe as an employee.

Now, there's nothing wrong with making someone else rich. I love making other people rich too. I just like to do it a different way. I like to make people rich through my business, not theirs.

If you're spending forty hours a week applying yourself to someone else's cause then you're essentially spending forty hours of your week focusing on making them money. But what about you in all this?

Wouldn't you prefer to spend those hours making yourself rich? Getting your business off the ground and flying high? Perhaps if you dedicated some time to your business, then you could make more people rich and give other people in a job.

Security is a big factor here. You can choose to make your life better with the ideas you have to create a business, which will create wealth and time, or you can continue working in a job, which will not really take you anywhere.

Having one million dollars in the bank does not need to be just a fantasy. However, many people believe that you must have that kind of money before you can achieve complete freedom in life.

You can do it, slowly and surely. Focusing on one thing at a time will help you become a master at it. As Confucius said, "The man who moves a mountain begins by carrying away small stones."

All you need to do is finally take the risk.

CHAPTER 5

MAKING YOUR MIND A MAGNET FOR SUCCESS

When I began entrepreneurship, I thought it would be easy. I thought that I would start to make money immediately, that I would have so much time on my hands and that life in general would be awesome. That was not the case at all. In fact, I started to doubt myself as I lost a lot of money investing in my business. I remember a time when I went to buy milk for my son and there was no money in my account. This scared me!

As my son was getting older and becoming more curious, I began to question my life choices again. I found that my wife was worried that I wasn't contributing enough emotionally to our growing family and that I was never home to spend time with them. I freaked out because deep down I knew it was true. I came home after my son had gone to bed for the night and I was out of the house before he left for school. So, I changed my scheduling around to spend more time with them and show them that they were my priority, not work.

I committed to waking up extra early to have time in the morning. I created a new habit and became more productive. I chose to meditate, exercise and plan my day accordingly. I also took more time to read inspirational literature to start my day. I took small steps to lead me into a healthier and more productive lifestyle that suited me and my growing family. I felt happier and more fulfilled. I realised that, in taking these small but powerful steps, my life was not only improving, but I was also matching the mindset of a millionaire.

These simple, small habits formed successful routines, and committing to these new routines changed my mindset and my life.

Adapting to a new set of healthy habits in itself can be daunting at first; however, repetition is key here. Once you get yourself into a good routine, you will find it easier to develop better habits, for example, saving money or getting rid of procrastination. This chapter is focused on building these important habits. They are the habits used by millionaires and billionaires.

The most important thing to discover is the journey to your own happiness. You are the author of your autobiography, you write the story of your life, no one can write your financial story and no one can write your spiritual or emotional journey. This is all up to you. Great habits help you get there. The power is within you.

STEP 3: CULTIVATE A MOVING-FORWARD MINDSET

Moving forward simply means—to progress.

You can change your mind but you might not be able to change your situation immediately—but you can impact your destiny by changing your actions and your mindset. One can never be successful with a fixed mindset.

People with a fixed mindset often believe that they cannot change because their traits and qualities are 'fixed'. They often choose not to work on developing or improving their skills or character because they believe that's the way they are. Period. Some people in this category have a deep believe that talent wins over hard work and therefore they choose not to ignite their inner resources to challenge that notion. In other words, they don't put in effort because they believe the one with 'natural talent' will succeed.

Those with a growth mindset are quite the opposite, they believe that they can improve with effort, education and training.

The terms I am using—'Growth Mindset' and 'Fixed Mindset' were first coined by leading researcher and psychologist Carol Dweck. Over 30 years ago, Carol Dweck became interested in students' attitudes about failure. Dweck and her colleagues noticed that some students quickly bounced back from perceived 'failures' while other students seemed very upset by small setbacks. Why did some students develop resilience and others didn't?

Dweck and her colleagues began to study how students unknowingly (or implicitly) assessed their own intelligence and abilities. They figured that how students deeply felt about their intelligence and abilities influenced their goals, motivations, behaviours, and self-esteem.

In other words, what students secretly believed about themselves influenced their behaviours.

To investigate this, they observed and studied students who were highly motivated to achieve, and students who were not. They noticed that the highly motivated students excelled when challenged while the less motivated students gave up or withdrew from their tasks.

They also discovered that a student's intelligence did not predict their levels of motivation.

They discovered that the two groups of students held different beliefs about their intelligence and abilities. And furthermore, it did affect their classroom performance.[2]

They studied the behaviour of thousands of children, and over time Dweck realised that individuals can be placed on a continuum according to their inner views of where ability comes from. Dr Dweck coined the terms **fixed mindset** and **growth mindset** to describe the underlying beliefs people have about learning and intelligence.

FIXED MINDSET — People who believe their success is based on their innate ability.

GROWTH MINDSET — People who believe their success is based on hard work, learning and training.

In her 2007 book *Mindset: The New Psychology of Success*, Dweck also said that people with growth mindsets "seem to have is a special talent for converting life's setbacks into future successes. Creativity researchers concur. In a poll of 143 creativity researchers, there was wide agreement about the number one ingredient in creative achievement. And it was exactly the kind of perseverance and resilience produced by the growth mindset."

---

2. Dweck, C.S.; Legget, E.L. (1988). "A social-cognitive approach to motivation and personality". *Psychological Review.* 95 (2): 256–273. doi:10.1037/0033-295x.95.2.256.

Your fixed beliefs will hold you back from making positive changes. Hence, it is essential to have a growth mindset/ winning mindset in order to push outside your comfort zone and persevere despite the obstacles.

HABITS YOU NEED TO CULTIVATE TO OBTAIN A GROWTH MINDSET

Acknowledge your weaknesses.

Weaknesses don't need to be hidden, you can bring them out into the open and work on them. Everyone has areas in life that aren't strengths. To cultivate a growth mindset it's important to accept you have some things you need to work on and get better at. We all have that in common. By accepting this and working on areas that aren't your strengths, you are already ahead of the game. Make small goals and step toward then in tiny steps. Give yourself the time and space you need to make progress, no matter how small it may seem. A growth mindset celebrates all the little steps. .

See obstacles as opportunities.

We are all faced with challenges and obstacles throughout life. Facing challenges head-on is part of developing leadership skills The more we stretch ourselves, the more we challenge ourselves. When we use obstacles as opportunities for learning and growth we become better, wiser and more resilient. New challenges and obstacles can in fact becomes new opportunities. Remember that science is now proving that our brains have the impressive ability to adapt and change throughout our entire life.

Your brain forms new connections when you are faced with new challenges, new environments and new opportunities. Neuroscience reveals that your brain can be rewired and retrained, which is great news because this means that there is always room for positive change. If you are aware that your brain is constantly changing, then you are more likely to adopt a growth mindset.

Remember that if the brain is not fixed, then the mind should not be fixed either.

Focus on yourself instead of approval.
A quick way to shut down an open and growth-orientated mindset is to make approval a priority. Approval seeking behaviour is a short road to nowhere. Let's be honest, no matter what you do, there are always a bunch of negative people that simply won't approve. It's an impossible game to win. So if you place learning and growing yourself and your business above any sort of approval — you're on the right track. A growth mindset adores learning and is willing to place it above a popularity contest. Don't worry about what other people think about you. Instead, focus on bettering yourself for your own benefit.

Be open to constructive criticism.
Constructive criticism is a wonderful way to learn about yourself. But it's different to just plain old criticism. The difference is that constructive criticism is about growing and finding ways to improve, criticism is often a personal complaint or offensive statement. It's important to learn how to take and deliver constructive criticism so that its understood as being well-intentioned and delivered in a positive way. It's important to not take it personally. If someone points a small fault of yours out, try and understand their intention behind it. Often they are really trying to help you see a blindspot. Constructive criticism can be a powerful tool for personal improvement.

Adapted from the work of Carol Dweck

Learn from the mistakes of others.

Comparing yourself to others can be detrimental to your growth. However, it is important to see that not everyone is perfect. If you identify another's mistake, take that as an opportunity to grow and learn for yourself.

Reflect on your learning every day.

Make sure you take some time every day to absorb as much information as possible. You can choose to write down in a little notebook, to research some new ideas, or to research a topic of interest to you. Don't let your most valuable lessons of the day be forgotten. Note them in a journal or at a minimum, sit with the idea of what you learned for a while and allow all the lessons to sink in.

In order to keep a growth mindset, it's important to understand how your mind can work for you. The subconscious mind is very powerful in helping you be your best.

Use the Power of Your Subconscious Mind

You must change any disempowering beliefs to make any positive changes. There are many things you can do to make things better for yourself. One of these things is to try NLP or Neurolinguistic Programming or self-hypnosis. Tools and techniques that help you will enter straight into the subconscious mind are very potent.

International renown scientists, Bruce H. Lipton, PhD and author of bestselling book *The Biology of Belief* explains the subconscious mind like this:

> *The two minds are the conscious and the subconscious. The conscious mind contains wishes and desires and operates about 5% of the time. That means that 95% of our lives are from the programs, which have been downloaded into the subconscious mind. Most of these programs are negative, disempowering, and self-sabotaging. While our conscious minds are busy thinking during the day, our subconscious programming self-sabotages. We externalize our struggles because we don't see that we're sabotaging ourselves; we only recognize that life isn't working.*[3]

---

3. Lipton PhD, Bruce. "How to Maintain the Infamous Honeymoon-Period-of-Bliss." Published blog online October 25, 2018. www.brucelipton.com/blog/how-maintain-the-infamous-honeymoon-period-bliss

So when you see that life isn't working for you, it's essentially saying that you need to get some new positive beliefs deep in your subconscious mind. You need to run new empowering mental programs.

He said, "The things that you like and that come easily to you in your life are there because you have a program that allows them to be there. In contrast, anything that you have to work hard at, put a lot of effort into or anything you have to struggle for to make it happen, is a result of your programs not supporting that."

Your mindset is vital in establishing a successful business and achieving your goals and living a fulfilling life.

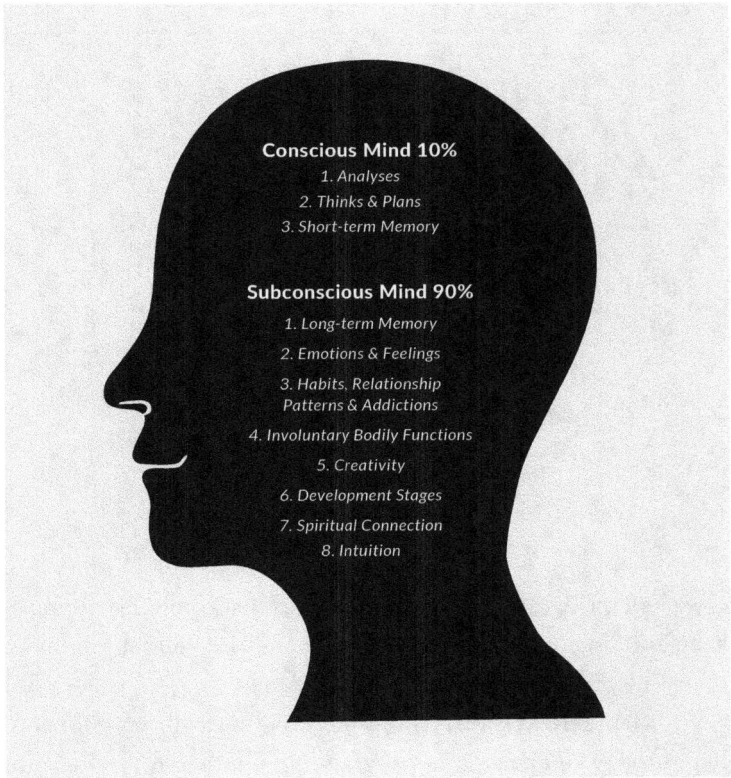

List some beliefs you would like to change about your mindset.

....

....

....

....

....

....

....

List all the things that come easy to you:
- ....
- ....
- ....
- ....
- ....

List all the things that are difficult for you:
- ....
- ....
- ....
- ....
- ....

For all the EASY THINGS—the things that come easy to you—keep building them—keep enjoying them. Use your strengths to their fullest potential.

For all the HARD THINGS—things that seem difficult for you. Begin today to change the programming, to begin to eradicate the blocks to success and erase the limiting beliefs so they do not grow anymore. You must visualise yourself as you wish to be.

Do the following exercise:

List 5 things you believe are difficult in starting your own business.

1. ....
2. ....
3. ....
4. ....
5. ....

List 5 things you believe are easy about entrepreneurship.

1. ....
2. ....
3. ....
4. ....
5. ....

How can you challenge your negative beliefs and enhance your positive beliefs?

....

....

....

....

Dr Bruce Lipton suggests that if you want to change a mental program, using "self-hypnosis" can be effective. As you go to bed, put on earphones to listen to positive visualisation programs that help you visualise your wishes and desires as you'd like to see them manifested in your life.

I strongly advocate to people to see themselves as they wish to be. Visualise yourself successful, talk successful, walk successful. Be successful in your mind FIRST!

VISUALISE YOURSELF AS YOU WISH TO BE

Visualising myself as I wanted to be in the future was a huge part of my transformation.

Visualisation has been long used in high-performance sport. For example, Roger Federer, one of the greatest tennis players in history visualises each match before he steps foot onto the court.

Champion surfer, Kelly Slater used visualisation to win major surfing tournaments. Famous sportspeople—Tiger Woods, Michael Jordan, Michael Phelps and many more have reported using visualisation to improve and drive their performance.

But it's not just for sport—people like Oprah Winfrey, Arnold Schwarzenegger and Jim Carrey all used visualisation to achieve success.

Natan Sharansky, a computer specialist who spent nine years in prison in the USSR after being accused of spying for the U.S., shows just what visualisation can do. While in solitary confinement, he played against himself in a mental game of chess. He said that he used "the opportunity to become the world champion!" And in fact, Sharansky beat the world champion chess player Garry Kasparov.

How to Visualise for Success

The first step to visualisation is to relax. Find a comfortable position and breathe deeply.

Now, imagine how you would like your life to be. What work are you doing? How are you dressed? What type of income are you earning? How is your life outside of work? See yourself happy and free.

The key is to make the pictures in your mind as bright and as vivid as you possibly can.

It doesn't matter if your life isn't like that yet. You can imagine anything your heart desires.

But to really succeed with visualisation, you must feel the same emotions that you would have if you had already had accomplished your goals.

Yes, feel the feelings as if it's already true for you.

Seeing the pictures in your mind is great but you have to penetrate your brain and body with the feelings you want.

Immerse yourself in these positive emotions. Experience exactly what you would experience if your dreams had come true. You will feel new feelings of joy, pride, success, wealth, confidence and happiness.

HOW TO VISUALISE
Follow the 3 easy steps below to start visualising.

1. FIND A PEACEFUL PLACE
The first step in visualisation is finding a peaceful place where you can be alone. You can choose:
- A nice shady tree at a park
- Your favourite spot at home
- Your private work office
- Anywhere you will not be distracted

2. CLEAR YOUR MIND
When preparing for visualisation, sit in a comfortable position.
- Close your eyes
- Relax and take some deep breaths
- Count down from 10 with each breath out and stay focused on your breathing
- Repeat until you feel clear and peaceful

3. IMAGINE YOUR GOALS
Visualise your goals with as many details as you can.
- Sights – What can you see?
- Sounds – What do you hear?
- Smells – What can you smell?
- People – Who is present?
- Write down your thoughts
- Create a vision board with your ideas

MORNING RITUALS TO STIMULATE ENERGY AND MOTIVATION

All successful entrepreneurs wake early because to do great things you need more time than others. Utilising the given 24 hours efficiently can give you all the time you want to do anything you want. As Richard Whately said, "Lose an hour in the morning, and you will be all day hunting for it."

Why are mornings powerful?
- You have more will-power in the morning
- You can take time out to make a schedule for the day and begin the day with positive thoughts and intentions
- Your brain is more active, and nothing distracts you.

The ongoing advantages to being an early-riser are plentiful. Most people find that they are more productive in the early hours of the morning and can seemingly fit more into their day. Essentially, it's like the ultimate head-start.

In fact, this has been backed by Christoph Randler, a biology professor at the University of Education in Heidelberg, Germany.

His research studies showed that early risers tend to be more proactive and productive.[4] He told the *Harvard Business Review* that, "When it comes to business success, morning people hold the important cards…Morning people also anticipate problems and try to minimize them, my survey showed. They're proactive. A number of studies have linked this trait, proactivity, with better job performance, greater career success, and higher wages."[5]

---

4. Randler, Christoph. (2009). Proactive People Are Morning People1. Journal of Applied Social Psychology. 39. 2787-2797. 10.1111/j.1559-1816.2009.00549.x.
5. Randler, Christoph, Defend Your Research: The Early Bird Really Does Get the Worm, *Harvard Business Review*, 2010, online article.

It's no wonder that people like Richard Branson, Indira Nooyi, and Anthony Robbins are early morning risers.

Apple mogul, Steve Jobs had his own morning routine. After he got up and was showered and dressed, he would head to his mirror and literally take a good look at himself. Steve Jobs would look at himself right in the eyes and ask, "If today was the last day of my life, would I be happy with what I'm about to do today?"

If he answered 'no' too many days in a row, he would ensure that things changed.

In a five-year study of self-made millionaires, Tom Corley author of *Rich Habits — The Daily Success Habits of Wealthy Individuals* found that almost 50 percent of them woke up at least three hours before their workday began.

Gratitude: Igniting the feeling of gratitude is often overlooked despite its power. It truly is one of the most positive and productive feelings you can muster. Cultivating an inner sense of thankfulness helps you to begin your day on the right foot, to spark a graciousness for all the good you already have in your life. And when you do this, you create even more good. When you focus on good things in your life, you feel more empowered and this electric, positive energy travels with you throughout the day.

Being thankful has been shown to have a lower risk in diagnoses like depression, anxiety and stress.

Gratitude has been associated with contributing to people feeling a higher sense of satisfaction in life. Research shows that gratitude is linked to psychological wellbeing—this means a sense of meaning in life.

Writing down your most important tasks: Don't let this little, practical ritual fool you with its simplicity — it's like pocket dynamite. When you begin your day by identifying and writing down your most important tasks for the day — you set yourself up for success. Write down one to three tasks that are essential for you to complete and get onto them early. These tasks support your long-term plans and dreams and will be the stepping stones toward your great success.

Listen to uplifting music: We all know that a great tune can change our mood. Listening to inspiring and uplifting music can charge you up for the day ahead. It energises you and pumps you full of happy feelings and cultivates a positive attitude. Being selective of the music you listen, deliberately choose beats and rhythms that inspire and delight you. There's no better way to start your day than by singing and dancing, right?

We can also alter our moods with the right type of music. High-performance athletes often use music to either calm nerves or motivate themselves. It's a natural mood-changer.

Music can also reduce depression and anxiety, and improve self-esteem and moods.

Music helps regulate emotions—so it can be a great idea to use music deliberately. Adam Sankowski from Harvard Medical Centre said, "Instead of listening to the music that matches your current mood try listening to the music that matches the mood that you want to be in."

Makes sense, right? Maybe use music to match your goals and future ambitions too. He says, "A basic guideline is to try to match the music to the mood that you want to have," he says. "If you need to get excited, listen to exciting music. Need to calm down? Listen to calming music."[6]

---

6. Utton, Dominic, Boost your mood with music: what to play throughout the day, *The Telegraph*, Feb 6, published online 2018.

CULTIVATE A MONEY-MAKING MINDSET

> *"Business money is limitless"*
> — *Muhammad Yunus*

Just about everybody wants to wealthy—so why do so few people get there?

Ask any wealthy person how they achieved financial independence and they won't say "it just happened". Wealth rarely happens by default or accident. Sure, some people win Tattslotto—but I wouldn't recommend relying on that.

It all starts with a plan, and a willingness to commit to that plan. It also takes a new way of thinking about money and your ability to make it.

Come up with your own version of what financial independence means to you—following someone else's definition may get you in trouble.

Thomas Corley, the author of *Rich Habits: The Daily Success Habits Of Wealthy Individuals* spent five years studying the lives of both rich people and poor people. Rich people were classified as having an annual income of $US160,000 or more and net worth of $US3.2 million or more and poor people were classified as having an annual income of $US35,000 or less and a liquid net worth of $US5,000 or less.

Corley believes that the key to success is to get "50% to be rich habits,"

In short—rich people:

- Set goals every day—and they put them in writing.
- Maintain a to-do list
- They don't waste money
- Watch less than one hour of TV per day
- They love to read—especially self-improvement and

industry-related books
- They listen to audio books
- They do more than their job requires
- They take risks
- Help others (Volunteer etc)
- They exercise regularly
- They have a "do it now" mindset
- Take care of themselves
- They listen 5x more than they talk
- Avoid toxic people
- Don't give up
- Have mentors
- They invest in relationships

> "Making money is a happiness. And that's a great incentive. Making other people happy is a super-happiness."
> — *Muhammad Yunus*

Set your financial goals:
First things first. Determine the approximate amount of money you need to have.

Know what you want to accomplish with this money over a period of time.

Identify the things you can let go of to save more.

Form a clear and effective strategy for saving and be determined to stick with it.

Be realistic:
Don't plan to save 50% of your earnings if the remaining amount is not even enough to fulfil your basic needs. This will impact you to the point where you are constantly withdrawing money from your savings in order to survive.

Also, be careful not to put yourself in a position where you are becoming so minimalistic that you end up becoming frustrated and give up on the whole idea of saving.

Come up with a realistic idea as to what you'll have to give up to get where you want to go. Have a realistic look at the obstacles in your path.

Be prepared to alter your lifestyle:
A financially demanding lifestyle will never let you save. If you spend most of what you earn and don't have control over your temptations, then you are still financially immature. Try to grow up, prioritise the things you really want to spend money on and forget the rest. If you cannot discipline yourself enough in this period, then you will never be able to succeed. This is the stage of growth and moving forward. It can be tough, but it is well worth it in the end.

If you are surrounded by people who prefer to spend their money frivolously and live and play hard—meaning they love to spend their money on fun rather than investing in themselves, you run the risk of getting pulled into their behaviour.

> *Too many people spend money they earned to buy things they don't want to impress people that they don't like.*
> — **Will Rogers**

Don't just save, invest:
Saving can be a very monotonous task if you don't see anything coming from it. So how do you take the stress out of saving? It's simple: *invest!* Even if you begin small, it can be quite an exciting time. Investing will also keep you motivated and, most importantly, you will see your money grow. This is the time to do some research, find a good financial advisor and invest in the

right places that suit your budget.

It's not always easy to build discipline in any area of your life. However, when you make the effort, the rewards are definitely worth it!

Cultivate The Goal-Setting Mindset

> *"You are not meant for crawling, so don't.*
> *You have wings. Learn to use them and fly."*
> **— Rumi**

A 2015 study by Professor of Psychology Gail Matthews from the Dominican University of California showed when people wrote down their goals, they were **33% more successful** in achieving them than those who formulated outcomes in their heads.[7]

So, we are going to do both. I am going to ask you to write down your goals and envision them in your mind too.

Set one major goal for the year.

Suppose your main goal for the next twelve months is to lay a foundation to begin your business. Focus on all the tasks necessary to start the business and don't think about anything else. Don't worry about leads, selling or growing. Just start. These goals will come later.

Think about it like this: Imagine yourself running a marathon. At the beginning, you pace yourself. If you run too fast at the beginning, you will tire too soon. It would be highly unlikely that you would finish the race if you start off this way. Hence, it is important to simply focus on the step you are taking right at this moment and forget the rest.

---

7. Gail Matthews, Professor, *Goals Research Summary*, Dominican University of California, 2015.

Annual Goal:

> *Impossible is just a word thrown around by small men who find it easier to live in the world they've been given than to explore the power they have to change it. Impossible is not a fact. It's an opinion. Impossible is potential. Impossible is temporary. Impossible is nothing.*
> — ***Muhammad Ali***

Manage your monthly goals to achieve your yearly goal.
You need to plan what you'll need to accomplish every month to keep you on track. Don't plan too many things. Start with one or two things, but make sure you do them. Don't skip any of your monthly tasks just because they're too complicated or you are procrastinating. Just try to do the things well on time with great zeal and determination. Also, have patience when a few tasks are taking longer to accomplish, as not everything will happen within the time frame you have predetermined. Just make sure that you take the time for each task per month. This way, they will all be done and your monthly goals will roll over into your yearly goal.

Monthly Goals

January: ....
....

February: ....
....

March: ....
....

April: ....
....

May: ....
....
....

June: ....

July: ....

August: ....

September: ....

October: ....

November: ....

December: ....

> *"Setting goals is the first step in turning the invisible into the visible."*
> **— Tony Robbins**

Plan your week according to your goals.

Keeping track of your monthly goals can be tough unless you know what you are doing each week. Little fractions of work become much more achievable than trying to take on the task as a whole. Your brain cannot perform optimally when it feels burdened or pressured. Make sure you are not over-loading yourself with work and are taking one day off a week to relax your mind. By doing this, you will be able to take on next week's tasks refreshed.

Weekly goals

Week 1: ....

....

Week 2: ....

....

Week 3: ....

....

Week 4: ....

....

Week 5: ....

....

Week 6: ....

....

Week 7: _____

_____

Week 8: _____

_____

Week 9: _____

_____

Week 10: _____

_____

Week 11: _____

_____

Week 12: _____

_____

Repeat.

Plan your daily activities.
The first and most important step to take towards working more efficiently is to have a daily plan in place. As you wake each morning, make a 'to do' list of things for the day. Check off the things you have done each time you complete them. This keeps your mind prepared for the task so you won't miss things that are important. Also, make sure that you

are not exerting yourself. Eat and sleep well and try to include some sort of exercise routine in your day. You will feel much better and will stay on track and healthy for work.

Daily Goals

Monday: ....

Tuesday: ....

Wednesday: ....

Thursday: ....

Friday: ....

Saturday: ....

Sunday: ....

You don't learn to walk by following the rules.
You learn by doing, and falling over.
— *Richard Branson*

Your work is going to fill a large part of your life, and the only way to be truly satisfied is to do what you believe is great work. And the only way to do great work is to love what you do.
— *Steve Jobs, Co-Founder and CEO, Apple*

CHAPTER 6

MY ENTREPRENEURSHIP JOURNEY

Now that I had a plan in place, I was more determined than ever to do whatever it took to grow my business and spend time with my family. I was focusing on the tasks at hand and putting my energy into growing my business. I made many mistakes along the way and then pulled myself back, took some time to reflect and started that task again. I found that I was networking—a lot. I was filling my time with meetings, attending a lot of workshops and simply spreading myself too thin. I was trying too hard.

SHINY OBJECT SYNDROME

Then I found a business coach. This was when I became aware that, by doing too much and spreading myself too thin, I was becoming a victim of an entrepreneurial syndrome: 'dabbler', or, in layman's terms, 'shiny object syndrome'. It's called shiny object syndrome because it's the entrepreneur's equivalent of a small child chasing after shiny objects. Once they get there and see what the object is, they immediately lose interest and start chasing the next thing.

I was constantly chasing after anything and everything that I thought would help me grow my business. As such, I was wasting time on things that simply did not work.

I took it upon myself to learn more about this syndrome. I discovered that the solution was to commit to one task at a time. Stop chasing. This was a wake-up call. I culled some things and stopped attending unnecessary meetings. This gave me more time to dedicate to the most important aspect of my business: developing a strong baseline.

The way you spend your time says a lot about your worth. You become what you spend your time on. If you have been working for someone without questioning why, you have become submissive. On the other hand, if you self-analyse, you will learn to spend time only on things that are essential for your development.

YOUR DEVELOPMENT

- What experiences have you had? How have these experiences impacted your growth?

MY ENTREPRENEURSHIP JOURNEY

- What are your talents? List at least five.

- What are your skills? Remember that *talents* are innate. Skills need to be worked on to perfect them.

- What are your strengths? How can you make the most of them?

- What do you want to do with your life?

- Are you happy with your health? If not, why not? And what can you do to move into wellness instead of living in sickness?

....
....
....
....
....
....
....
....
....
....
....
....
....

- What makes you feel fulfilled?

....
....
....
....
....
....
....
....

- What is important to you? Are you spending time on things that are important for your growth?

....
....
....
....
....
....
....

TO DEVELOP FURTHER...

Know your worth

You will never be paid what you are worth working for someone else. Getting to know what you are worth takes time and practice. Do not sell yourself short. Take these next steps to determine where you stand.

> *When you know your worth, no one can make you feel worthless.*
> — ***Anonymous***

Understand the power of your attitude towards yourself

How do you feel about yourself deep down? Do you value yourself and care about your success and happiness? It's important to think about how you perceive yourself, because ultimately, what we believe about ourselves is what we become. Putting yourself down and telling everyone about all your faults doesn't do much good for your self-worth or self-esteem. This doesn't mean of course that you inflate yourself and become egotistical or arrogant either, it simply means that you genuinely care for yourself in a way that you would others. Begin to cultivate a supportive attitude towards yourself, one that is caring and encouraging, one that helps you rather than hinder you. The small shifts in attitude end up making the mightiest differences in the long run.

Learning to talk yourself in a more positive way may feel uncomfortable at first, but with a little time and effort, you can alter your low self-worth and bring it up to a better level, a level than is authentic and powerful. After all, whose job is it to raise your SELF worth and esteem? Your-SELF, right?

> *Until you value yourself, you won't value your time. Until you value your time, you will not do anything with it.*
> *— M. Scott Peck*

Trust your own feelings

We have all had moments of self-doubt, it's a feeling that we have all experienced at some time or another. But where self-doubt becomes a real problem if when we say stuck in it and become untrusting of our own feelings. Self-doubt is like a poison, if you keep swallowing it, it kills you. It stops you from being your best and from living your best life.

Building trust yourself is critical to success, when you can rely on yourself — you're in control. When you can trust your own feelings you can recognise when things seem off or not quite right. You will build a bond between your instincts and knowledge and learn to validate your internal intuitions.

Your sense of worth plummets when you listen to other people's feelings ahead of your own. You have an inbuilt system that is wired to look after you and protect you from danger — it's important to form a new relationship with it. With yourself.

Don't always let other people decide what you should do or what way is best for you. You decide! You know yourself better than anyone. Remember, you have lived with yourself you're entire life. Stand up for yourself and realise that you have a voice that can be heard too. Value yourself as someone important and worthwhile. You don't need to dance to someone else's beat when you can play your own percussion.

Make decisions that support YOU. Make life choices that serve YOU. Don't be afraid to take your life by the horns and make it work—your way.

Always trust your gut feelings, as they never lie the way people do.
— *Anonymous*

STEP 4: MAXIMISE YOUR TIME AND WORTH

10 WAYS TO MAKE THE MOST OF YOUR TIME AND MAXIMISE YOUR WORTH

1. Avoid juggling too many things at once.

Trying to juggle too many things at one time is for professional jugglers in the circus. It takes a lot of concentration and can only be sustained for a short amount of time. Multi-tasking as a habit isn't a good long-term approach. When we try to do too many things at once, we lose engagement and productivity. It's better to do one thing at a time well than try to tackle multiple things and do none of them well.

Scientists at the Institut National de la Santé et de la Recherche Médicale (INSERM) in Paris revealed that multitasking didn't work. They asked a group of people to complete two tasks at the same time while they recorded their brain activity under fMRI resonance imaging machines. The results showed very interesting results. The people's brains had to try and split tasks causing them to forget details and make three times more mistakes.[8]

If you need a clear map to know what to focus on time management, there is a formulation called the The Eisenhower Method.[9] It helps you in categorising tasks into whether they are urgent or important. It clears up what you should focus on and when, recognising that important tasks may not be urgent, and urgent tasks are not necessarily important.

	URGENT	NOT URGENT
IMPORTANT	Quadrant I: Urgent & Important DO	Quadrant II: Not Urgent But Important PLAN
NOT IMPORTANT	Quadrant III: Urgent But Not Important DELEGATE	Quadrant IV: Not Urgent & Not Important ELIMINATE

8. Charron S, Koechlin E. Divided representation of concurrent goals in the human frontal lobes. Science. 328(360), 360-363 (2010).
Clapp W, Rubens M, Sabharwal J, Gazzaley A. Deficit in switching between functions underlies the impact of multitasking memory in older adults. Proceedings of the National Academy of Sciences of the United States of America. 108(17), 7212-7217 (2011).
9. McKay; Brett; Kate (October 23, 2013). "The Eisenhower Decision Matrix: How to Distinguish Between Urgent and Important Tasks and Make Real Progress in Your Life". *A Man's Life, Personal Development.*

2. Don't pay attention to every email alert.

You don't need to jump to attention every time an email hits your inbox. Every time a little 'ding' sounds to indicate that an email has hit your inbox—you don't need to check it like the email police. If you create a habit like this it sets you up to always be at the mercy of your email inbox, and we all know that inboxes only keep filling up with more stuff.

Try to set times where you check your emails. For example, perhaps you can check them once in the morning and once in the afternoon. Or perhaps you can create a fixed routine of three times per day, 9am, 1pm and 5pm only. This sets you up to control your inbox rather than have your inbox controlling you. People will become accustomed to the way that you operate and even respect you for it. Pointless emails are just that—pointless. But your important emails will be addressed at your pre-determined times.

Studies show the average professional spends about 28% of the day emailing. Inspired by that statistic, Gloria Mark and Stephen Voida from the University of California, Irvine, studied an office environment where 13 employees were cut off from email for an entire five days. They wore heart monitors and tracked their computer use. The result? The employees were less stressed when cut off from their email. They were able to focus for longer periods of time and minimised their multitasking efforts, which made them more productive.[10]

3. Scrolling social media without a purpose.

It's no surprise that social media can be a major distraction for many people. In fact, for some it's an addiction. There's a difference with using social media or letting social media

---

10. Mark, Gloria, Gudith, Daniela, Klocke, Ulrich, 2008/01/01, The cost of interrupted work: More speed and stress – 10.1145/1357054.1357072. Conference on Human Factors in Computing Systems – Proceedings

use you. If you're using valuable work time to scroll through pointless social media posts, then you're basically allowing the biggest time-sucking parasite to destroy your hard work. If you use social media to help you get sales and elevate your business, then that's different. It's useful.

Social media can be effective if you use it effectively. Scrolling pointless posts that don't relate to your personal or business growth may be a good way to relieve stress or "tune out" to the real issues but as a long-term approach it will put a huge dent in your time.

Imagine how many hours you could spend on laser-focused action in your business instead of checking your posts or counting your followers? Don't let the "social" in social media become your main focus. Use it as a tool to grow and enhance your business, not for wasting your valuable time.

4. Meetings for the sake of it.

Meetings are great environments for sharing information and making decisions. The problem is when meetings become redundant and happen without a purpose. When meetings happen for the sake of it. Time spent in directionless meetings are pointless. Time spent in directional meetings are valuable. Think about the time it takes to have a meeting, to prepare a meeting, to take the minutes of a meeting and to follow-up the agenda from the meeting. You have to consider prior to any meeting — what is the cost, what is the purpose and what is the point of the meeting. If it's necessary—go all in. If not, cancel it and get some work done.

A study conducted by the University of Nebraska[11] found

---

11. Yoerger, Michael; Crowe, John; and Allen, Joseph A., "Participate or Else!: The Effect of Participation in Decision-Making in Meetings on Employee Engagement" (2015). Psychology Faculty Publications. 120. https://digitalcommons.unomaha.edu/psychfacpub/120

that unproductive meetings costs companies time, morale and money. That's a big price to pay for not getting things done!

Make sure your meetings are meaningful and matter. Give them a direction and get things accomplished. After all, isn't that the idea of meetings? .

5. Declutter your work environment.

Does your desk look like a bomb went off? Is it piled with papers and notes and endless 'to-do' lists? Are your items scattered everywhere? Do have old filing in one big heap that you simply haven't had time to put away?

Disorganised desks usually belong to disorganised minds. Not only is your desk messy but it makes you mind messy too. You never feel totally in control. Take time (even if you're busy) to declutter your work area. File things away. Make it ergonomic and organised. Create a work space that empowers you rather than one that makes you feel overwhelmed. You'll become more productive and you'll feel fantastic about the work that you do. If you want to be a professional, then make your environment professional too. Even if you only have a corner of your home as your office — make it a powerful and professional place to work from.

6. Avoid being the social butterfly at work.

If you work with other people it's important to be friendly and build great relationships. However, being an active social butterfly when you need to be knuckling down and working just annoys everyone. There's a healthy balance between working well and forming good relationships. When a social butterfly within the group makes it their business to chit-chat to everyone instead of getting the job done, it creates an unproductive culture. Using breaks or lunch to catch up is a better idea. If you work by yourself that doesn't mean you're exempt. Phone calls or video conferences also have their social butterflies. Networking and building relationships at work is vital to success, just be aware that this doesn't tip over to being the excessive talker that drains healthy productivity.

7. Stop trying to figure out everything yourself.

Imagine that you get offered to be in charge of a big project. It's the chance you've been looking for to highlight your skillset. You're confident that you can do it. However over time the demands become huge and your realise that you've bitten off more than you can chew. You begin to panic. Instead of asking for more resources or help, you try to figure everything out yourself. You don't ask for help in case people may think you're incapable of tackling the big project.

Instead of getting answers and solutions from outside, you let personal pride rule the day. In order to be the most productive, you may need to seek help sometimes. You don't need to be the business martyr and handle everything yourself if you can't. To be the most time-efficient person you can be, you have to know when to push through and when to delegate or collaborate.

8. Pay attention to your wellbeing.

Burnout is a real thing. In fact it's now becoming a silent epidemic. Many people are working long hours and find themselves in a state of chronic stress. If you find yourself constantly exhausted and chronically stressed, you can't be your best. I did this for way too long and it ends in a downward spiral of ill-health and mental exhaustion.

In order to be successful, you must take care of yourself. Make sleep and eating well a priority. If you're not well, you can't stay productive. There have been so many scientific studies about workplace wellbeing and mental health. Basically, to perform well, you must take care of your physical and mental wellbeing.

9. Have direction every day.

If you want to maximise your time and worth, you must set clear intentions every day. Have a direction every day. What do you want to achieve? What direction are you taking? Are you heading toward your goals or away from them?

Don't just let the day take you where it decides. You must be in charge of your own day, your own time, your own direction. Don't let your days happen by chance. Seize the day! Write down what you want to accomplish and set your eyes on productive tasks. A little direction every day pays incredible dividends.

10. Shift from scarcity to abundance

In order to get started in your business and keep it going, it is essential to shift from a scarcity mindset to an abundance mindset when it comes to money. An abundance mindset helps you to be open with each of your financial options and situations.

When you start a new business venture it's difficult to not worry about things. Will you have the money to support yourself? Will you be able to make it work? Try and switch to an abundant mindset that isn't delusional. Decide how many customers you need to support your business and go out there and find them. They exist everywhere in abundance, but you need to find them. Don't let fear cripple your dreams, become filled with an abundance mindset and get active in pursuit of your dreams. You must make your goals bigger than your fears. You must take action towards abundance.

So, how can you begin to pivot your mindset from scarcity to abundance? Let's look.

WAYS TO SHIFT FROM SCARCITY TO ABUNDANCE

Your money needs a growth plan

Nearly everyone has heard people experts about budgeting. I am not talking about budgeting your money (though that does have a place). I am talking about making an abundance plan for your money. You must give your money a purpose and direction toward growth. If you don't plan for your money to grow, it won't happen by default. Abundant thinkers know that money grows. That it's not fixed and inactive. Money is a dynamic force that can grow and expand with you.

Don't buy stuff you don't need

Many people like to consume stuff they don't need. There's a great quote that says, "Too many people spend money they haven't earned to buy things they don't want to impress people they don't like." Abundance isn't about consuming more stuff or impressing people with your wealth. True abundance isn't about maxing out your credit card so you can have the latest furniture in your home. Abundance isn't about going into mass debt to look like you've "made it." True abundance is a feeling of knowing there's enough and being grateful for the goodness that is everywhere.

Don't compare yourself to others

This is a common trap. Comparing what you do or don't have against other people isn't smart. There will always be people poorer and richer than you. If you waste your time comparing yourself with others, you'll always believe that what you have isn't enough. And that's not true. Scarcity thinkers always believe that they don't have enough, or what they do have isn't as good as someone else. Celebrate your own abundance goals.

If you see someone that you know has just purchased a new car and you feel envious, you don't know what is happening behind the scenes. Maybe they went into debt to get it. Maybe they have to work harder now just to keep their fancy new car. Abundance is about celebrating abundance. Try to avoid feeling resentful or jealous of what other people have. There is enough for everyone and just because someone else has something, doesn't mean that you miss out. Try to have a mindset that supports money and lets it flow to everyone.

SCARCITY

Believes in — I win/you lose

Believes there's not enough to go around

Feels envy, comparison and anxiety

Says, "I'll never be rich."

Is suspicious of others

Believe that money is hard to get

Is scared of change

Avoids risk

Competes for the prize

Doesn't trust collaboration

Blames circumstances or people

Feels that everything is a struggle

ABUNDANCE

Believes in win-win scenarios

Happy to collaborate

Knows that money expands and grows

Is comfortable with change

Takes risks

Believes there is enough for everyone

Takes responsibility for financial wealth

Sees opportunities for growth

Optimistic about future goals

Builds great relationships

Enjoys flow and ease

Believes in teamwork and giving

Ask yourself:
- What are your beliefs about money?

- What can you say or do to help move from scarcity to abundance?

Make a list of 'Abundance Affirmations'.
Here are some to get you started.
- » The best is yet to come
- » Every day I am getting better and better
- » My income is constantly expanding
- » I welcome wealth and prosperity
- » I share myself freely
- » I am optimistic about the future
- » I am a money magnet
- » I enjoy more freedom each day
- » Life is good for me and my family
- » I am secure and happy

Now add some more of your own:

"Every worthwhile accomplishment, big or little, has its stages of drudgery and triumph: a beginning, a struggle and a victory."
*— **Mahatma Gandhi***

Hemi is sharing more in his INTERACTIVE book.

See exclusive, behind-the-scenes videos, audios and photos.

DOWNLOAD free content and learn how to Grow With Hemi.

growwithhemi.com/interactive

CHAPTER 7

THE PROXIMITY PRINCIPLE

It didn't take me long to get into a powerful morning routine. I would meet lots of different people who had a similar work ethic and similar interests. I realised that these people were highly successful and belonged to an elite society of financial professionals working at a very fast pace. I questioned how they got to be where they are, and I began to understand what it took to be a successful entrepreneur.

I began to see improvements in my work. I felt more motivated than ever. I attended some more empowering workshops, which were extremely insightful. I ended up joining a coach success program. During the classes, we would discuss the issues we faced as entrepreneurs. While there, I learned the ins-and-outs of how to gain mental and financial freedom to create stability in my business and in my life.

I found that being around these people instead of in a company filled with employees trying to make ends meet changed my perception on how to create growth in my life. Instead of discussing how hectic my life was, I was now discussing how I was going to achieve great wealth and a happy lifestyle.

STEP 5: USE THE PROXIMITY PRINCIPLE

Proximity is power. The simplest and most vital way to realise your dream goals faster is by placing yourself in proximity of people who have already reached their goals and are doing better than you are at the moment. Proximity is power!

How Does It Work?

Proximity gives you the ability to capitalise your growth by modelling strategies in your business that are proven to work, thereby eliminating the time that is uselessly consumed by trial and error. When you watch successful people closely and mingle with them, you effortlessly begin to replicate their actions. This brings you closer to success.

If you see someone who succeeds all the time, luck has nothing to do with it. It all comes down to strategy. Not once, not twice, but every time? That does not mean they are lucky. It means they have a strategy that works. Take notice of that.

Who Do You Mix With?

In order to become successful, it is important to know who to mix with. Their influence will inform the actions you take to create more success. It is believed that, on average, you are influenced most by the five closest people you mingle with. Therefore, if you want to be successful, you must reassess who you are spending your time with and choose to spend more time with successful people.

The positive influence of the successful people in your life will give you an inspirational and motivational mindset. Following their behaviours, applying their top strategies and knowing how they produce a desired result can make your work easier and more effective.

Mixing with successful people does not always mean that you have to physically meet them or be with them. All it means is that you keep track of what they are doing, how they are doing it and what lessons they have to teach you through their work. You can be in proximity of a successful person by reading their books, listening to their podcasts, following their personal, company profiles, and so on. You just have to make them a part of your life so that you can live life successfully.

This says it all:

> *Surround yourself with people that push you to do better. No drama or negativity. Just higher goals and higher motivation. Good times and positive energy. No jealousy or hate. Simply bringing out the absolute best in each other.*
> **— *Warren Buffet***

Make a list of some people you could begin to associate with. And people to avoid.

Investigate meetings or networks you could join that have a track system of success.

How Do You Choose Your Business Partner?

When you select a business partner, you must be sure that you both have the same energy and synergy. You must also both have a similar vision for the business and similar skills. In your initial conversation on day one, be clear about the rules and responsibilities of all parties involved.

Where Should You Go To Learn?

Commencing a new business can be really tough. It is essential to gain some knowledge in the field and obtain some skills to keep your boat afloat. But the sad fact is that not every book you read will give you knowledge that helps your business grow. Some strategies you learn will not apply to your business very well. You need strategies for the situations that your business is facing. One way to come with up with the strategies that your business needs is to seek help from successful business coaches, who have a path to get your business on the right track.

Webinars and workshops are a great way to gain new skills that are essential to the growth of your business. You can use YouTube and podcasts to learn and grow. Books are a brilliant resource. Global mogul and billionaire, Warren Buffet, is an avid reader. He shares that reading books helps him improve his decision making and gain clarity in his thoughts.

Regardless of your business status, hiring a business coach can accelerate your business. They can give you new tools and share their wisdom to help you avoid a lot of the common pitfalls. They are experts at helping your business grow, at the same time they also grow you.

> *"Not all readers are leaders, but all leaders are readers."*
> *— Harry Truman*

Who To Learn From?

There are many free online learning platforms, and a plethora of videos, articles, webinars, podcasts and books available. I personally still use many of these platforms to continue my knowledge and growth. When I first started, and even few years back, I hired a business coach for myself. A business coach can make you accountable and support your goals and endeavours with sage and proven advice.

Based on their own experiences, ten successful founders from the *Young Entrepreneur Council (YEC)* discuss some of the benefits of hiring a business coach.[12]

1. **You'll go outside your comfort zone** (Dave Nevogt, Hubstaff.com)

2. **You'll get personal attention from someone who knows your business inside and out** (Beck Bamberger, BAM Communications)

3. **You'll finally have someone who isn't afraid of correcting you** (Marc Devisse, Tri-Town Construction)

4. **You'll learn how to make your ideas a reality** (Miles Jennings, Recruiter.com)

5. **You'll gain a needed confidante** (Charlie Gilkey, Productive Flourishing)

6. **Your networking opportunities will skyrocket** (Drew Gurley, Redbird Advisors)

7. **You'll make more money** (Derek Hunter, William Roam)

8. **You'll develop self-confidence** (Jon Tsourakis, Revital Agency, LLC)

9. **You'll be held accountable for what really matters** (Jeff Cayley, Worldwide Cyclery)

10. **You'll hear unbiased opinions** (Brittany Hodak, ZinePak)

---

12. Young Entrepreneur Council (YEC) – https://yec.co

CHAPTER 8

DIGITAL DOMINANCE

I was going along quite well on my ongoing entrepreneurship journey. I had developed a few businesses with good earnings, but I still was not living the life I wanted. I was not earning enough money to get the freedom I desired in life. I started to doubt myself again and felt trapped (again).

My wife got pregnant for the second time and she was planning to take maternity leave. I started to feel shaky as her income would then cease. I was not sure I would be able to continue with my entrepreneurship journey. As I've mentioned before, I always like to step back and analyse the situation. I have found many entrepreneurs don't do this and they constantly try the same things and fail.

I went to my coach and worked with him to work on some solutions. I concluded that I was not getting enough clients because my marketing was not good enough. Without proper strategies, I was wasting my money on social media and it wasn't providing results.

I love to learn before undertaking anything. I enrolled in a digital marketing course and took it very seriously. I started to research everything about digital marketing and social media. I was obsessed with gathering more knowledge about this.

STEP 6: USE THE POWER OF DIGITAL MARKETING

People are now moving away from traditionally crafted television ads, radio spots, telephone book listings, yellow pages, magazine and newspaper ads, brochures, and so on. Businesses are now trying to reach out to millions, indeed billions, of prospective customers with the help of multiple electronic options through digital marketing tools within Facebook, Instagram, Twitter, Google+, YouTube, e-mails, blogs, corporate websites, and so on.

Wikipedia describes digital marketing as "marketing of products or services using digital technologies on the Internet, including through mobile phone apps, using display advertising, and any other digital mediums.

Digital marketing channels are systems based on the internet that can create, accelerate, and transmit product value from producer to the terminal consumer by digital networks."

It is not that digital marketing has made print media marketing obsolete. Print media marketing will continue to exist alongside digital marketing, in a similar way to the co-existence of printed books and e-readers, where the same person swaps between different modes of reading. However, with time, internet marketing will continue to take centre stage because it offers quite a few advantages compared to print marketing.

Digital is now dominate. In fact, digital is here to stay and there's nothing you can do about it except jump on board.

Just recently, global company Unilever has created a new job role of 'chief digital and marketing officer' as it looks to become a "future-fit, fully digitised organisation."

More major companies are following this path.

According to research conducted by Cisco, at least 40% of businesses will die if they don't accommodate new technologies.

In this day and age, we must adapt, embrace the digital age and learn to thrive in it.

Further research conducted by Gartner indicated that:

- By 2021, more than 50% of enterprises will be spending more per annum on bots than app development
- By 2022, 40% of customer-facing employees will use some form of daily AI virtual support system.[13]

The age of technology will give many opportunities to those who keep up with it and stay educated about its rapid changes.

Many people feel they will lose their jobs to AI and robots, but according to research conducted by McKinsey, over the next 10 years, there will be more jobs created than destroyed. This is because AI and automation won't eradicate jobs but instead we will work alongside it and use it as part of our work.

It is believed that about 80% of jobs will experience some form of task automation.

I believe we best be ready, skilled and equipped to handle these changes so when they come we get the opportunity to flourish.

WHY DIGITAL?

By 2021, it's projected that marketing leaders will spend 75% of their total marketing budget on digital marketing, rather than traditional marketing.[14]

Besides the economic benefits and the fact everything will be digitally dominating it also offers:

» Flexibility – you can work anytime, anywhere, all around the world

---

13. Gartner, Gartner Top Strategic Predictions for 2020 and Beyond, published online October 22, 2019.
14. Salesforce Research, *2016 State of Marketing Report*: Trends and insights from nearly 4,000 marketing leaders worldwide.

- » As it keeps evolving, it gives you the chance to upskill and alter your approach
- » It gives you new skills and therefore new advantages in the job market
- » It gives you the option of regular revamping, knowing your market, and creating links.
- » It gives you the chance to operate your own business

I have come up with few a few flexibility factors that digital marketing offers, which I believe provide compelling reasons for why we should make use of it.

REVAMP

A regular revamping is necessary for your website. It is also easy. It does not cost much to give the website a complete makeover, especially when compared with the cost of a revamped, re-branded print ad for your company. With some tweaking you can create a new feel and look for your website, giving it new branding and style.

WATCH THE WATCHERS

You can easily identify your market by carefully viewing who is watching your online marketing ads. These people might not always be your target audience, but they are the ones who are interested in your product or service. It is a great opportunity for any business to leverage that interest. From this, you might also perform an analysis on how to attract more people, and thereby reconsider your campaign positioning. Once you identify and gather information about who is responding to your digital marketing, you are in a better position to target this regular online audience by adjusting your campaign to their taste.

LINKING

Digital marketing is a meaningful way to foster a link between business and customer. Regular blog posts, updates, tweets and Facebook posts give customers updates about the service. Moreover, the reaction of the audience allows the company to receive meaningful insights into the customers' needs and opinions. This interaction enables the company to adapt their services to meet the requirements of the customers, thereby increasing sales and profits. Using video and audio can be useful too—adding a product video on your landing page can increase conversions by 80% according to landing page experts Unbounce.

EVERYONE IS EQUAL

Whether you are a small, medium or large sized business, digital marketing platforms treat your business the same way. You can conduct as aggressive a marketing campaign as any large business, irrespective of the size of your organisation. Creativity and technical know-how help in conducting effective digital marketing. There are also many digital marketing platforms that enable smaller companies to market with a limited budget but with the effectiveness of a well-funded company.

LOCAL IS GLOBAL

Irrespective of where you are located and what the time of day is, you can conduct your digital marketing campaign anytime, anywhere and reach a global audience. No longer do you have to pay extra for international advertising. Instead, pay and work locally and reach the millions and billions out there in the world. You have the option of working as many hours and days as you want—or of taking a few days off to relax.

Every entrepreneur struggles to bring new leads to their business. But we think we know what to do about marketing. Trust me, I was in the same boat. Now, however, I know what to do, and my business has seen massive growth, ever since I learned about digital marketing.

BUILD HABITS OF A DIGITAL ENTREPRENEUR

Nowadays, many people don't stop at a single job for very long; they do not like the concept of becoming stagnant. They move from job to job because they want to gain experience, add something 'new' to their resume, that's what they love to do. They understand the importance of passion. Without passion for work, it's hard to concentrate, so they always find something that fits with their passion.

Often, we can see a lot of successful people around us, people who have been able to achieve what they have desired by following their passion. These people have decided to do something unique, not walk the conventional path, not work under someone, but be their own boss. Working for someone is a passé for them; rather, their success theory is work for yourself. Like these people, we too can dream of creating the next Pathao, Uber, AirBnB or Chaldal. It's not just about making money anymore. It's all about doing what we love and following our passion. With the help of digital marketing you can combine your skills and passion too.

This digital era has created a lot of opportunities for us. It is easier than ever to create and build an audience and grow a business. To succeed in this field, we need to understand its ecosystem and learn how to evolve with it. Without adopting this trend and following the footsteps of the successors, your next "big" concept might just be a redundant idea. To become a successful digital entrepreneur, we need to inculcate a few habits that successful digital entrepreneurs have.

7 INSPIRING HABITS OF A SUCCESSFUL DIGITAL ENTREPRENEUR

Flexibility of mindset

> *"The difficulty lies not so much in developing new ideas as in escaping from old ones."*
> — **John Maynard Keynes**

Yes, it's true, and we have to be free from all old habits. If something is not working, stop doing it again and again, rather innovate something new, or change your tactic.

Not afraid of failure

Our mindset often associates failure as a negative word, but for a digital entrepreneur, you have to consider failure as a badge of honour. You will be astonished to hear the number of failures successful businesses and entrepreneurs faced. To succeed, they have changed their business and business models. So don't be afraid of failure, just remember to learn from them to do better the next time.

Build business agility

Large and traditional organisations are like big ships; they need a lot of time to take a turn. For a small business as a digital entrepreneur, you have the ability to change an idea fast. For example, if something is not working, like a Facebook ad is not providing the expected leads or a landing page is broken, change it ASAP. A successful digital entrepreneur always welcomes change.

Adopt new tools
Always find new tools before your competitors get them and use them. New tools are coming into the market on a regular basis. Use them wisely for automation, segmentation and lead generation.

Develop digital hustle
If you think you can build a business and consumers will just instantly arrive at your door and buy, then think again. You have to be smart enough to bring audiences to you and work on your business and tactics to promote it. A digital entrepreneur must learn ways to grow a business within a small marketing budget.

Know the importance of digital assets
In the 'old business' concept, factories, offices and showrooms are considered assets of a company. Nowadays, it has changed. No longer is a business purely defined by its physical assets. It is the knowledge of economics, web traffic, emails and leads, which are the true assets for a digital entrepreneur.

Ideas for free
Previously, sharing a business model with someone was considered dangerous for your business. Digital entrepreneurs reject this idea and often shares its different platforms with other people. The entrepreneur also receives constructive criticism from different domains that help them develop their businesses further.

QUESTIONS TO PONDER:

- Do you believe that preparation and strategy are important? Why? Why not?

- What are your thoughts about marketing? How much money would you spend for marketing to bring leads to your business?

- What do you know about marketing?

- Do you feel you could learn more about marketing in the digital world?

- How will you go about making this happen for yourself?

- What is your marketing strategy right now?

- Do you believe that everything is digital?

- How can you develop 'digital hustle'?

"I'm convinced that about half of what separates the successful entrepreneurs from the non-successful ones is pure perseverance."
— Steve Jobs, Co-Founder and CEO, Apple

CHAPTER 9

TRANSFORM & PERFORM:
THE 9 POINT BUSINESS STRATEGY

*"Even the greatest was once a beginner.
Don't be afraid to take that first step."*
— *Muhammad Ali*

Entrepreneurship is not an easy journey. We all need to develop a clear strategy from the beginning.

I have learned from life that the major factors in success are discipline and strategy. I didn't learn it from bookish theories. Rather, I learned it from years of experience, trial and error, and sleepless nights—all of which I eventually overcame by compiling the lessons I learned and applying them to my life. In most cases, people are aware of the importance of discipline and strategy. However, they don't consistently make them their focus. In the journey of entrepreneurship, where you are the captain of your own ship, they are especially important, because, without vision and strategy, you will not be able to face and survive the storms.

Realising this, I have developed a unique 9P Business Strategy to help people who want to take the path of entrepreneurship. If you are an experienced business owner who is not getting the results they expected, paying attention to these strategies will help give you clarity of thought and aid you in devising the right business strategies.

Through all my years of trial and error, I have come up with a proven formula that will increase sales and help you to achieve your goals faster and more efficiently than you would have on your own.

STEP 7: TRANSFORM AND PERFORM

THE 9P BUSINESS STRATEGY

1. Perspective
2. Passion
3. Pain
4. People
5. Positioning
6. Prepare
7. Product
8. Promote
9. Profit

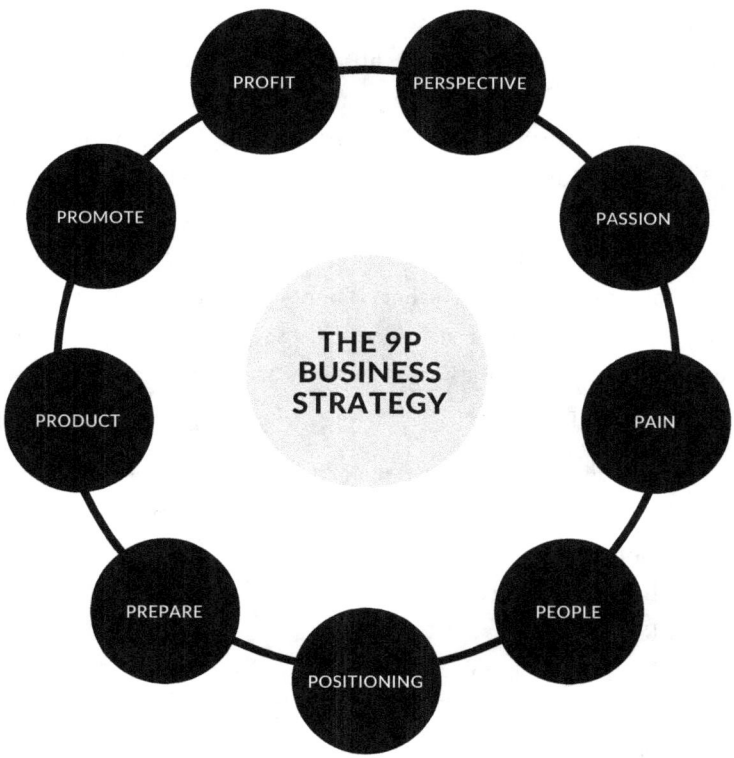

1. Perspective

*"When you get stronger everything in the world gets easier.
Change yourself and you've changed everything."*
— Hunter Post

Often when we talk about entrepreneurship or entrepreneurial growth, we narrow it down to sales objectives, hiring the right talent and other such objectives, but often we miss the most important factor: **perspective**.

In entrepreneurship, perspective is about having the mindset of an entrepreneur. As Robert Kiyosaki says: "True success does not come from money and opportunity but what you do with it."

In fact, mindset is most often the dividing line between those who are successful in life and those who are not. You have heard my story on how changing my mindset changed my life, and I want you to try it out. It is important to have the mindset of an entrepreneur rather than that of an employee. It may be a new shift but it's worth it.

Some might have the perspective of an entrepreneur from the beginning, whereas others might develop it. But in both cases the mindset of a successful entrepreneur cannot be created overnight. Rather, it is a process that needs to be nurtured over time.

Often, when you do not have the mindset of a successful entrepreneur or have a positive mindset you will suffer from:

- Confusion
- Lack of courage
- Regrets
- Non-appreciation of time, relationships, jobs
- Dissatisfaction
- Negativity
- Self-doubt

All these can lead to frustration and challenges in everyday life.

With the right perspective you will develop the skills to view your path clearly and have the courage to follow your dreams and ambitions. As Napoleon Hill said, "There are no limitations to the mind except those we acknowledge. Both poverty and riches are the offspring of thought."

With the positive attitude, you will have the ability to pull yourself out of the trap of regret and self-doubt. A positive mindset that you can be a successful entrepreneur will develop more and more within you. This will enable you to propel yourself forward. This mindset might dim, once you become entrenched in the daily routine of being an entrepreneur, but it is important that you make the effort to hone this entrepreneurial perspective so you can meet your everyday goals and challenges and enjoy your growth.

> "Be so committed to your dreams that naysayers will stop discouraging you and simply move out of your way."
> **— Nicky Verd**

Add your own perspectives here:

My perspectives for my business are: ....

....

....

....

....

....

My perspectives for my life are: ....

....

....

....

....

....

2. Passion

> *"If you have a strong purpose in life, you don't have to be pushed. Your passion will drive you."*
> **— Roy T. Bennett**

In the everyday grind of our lives, we often forget what our passion is. But to be a successful entrepreneur—or even to live your life to the fullest—it is important to remember what your passion is. As an entrepreneur, there is nothing more satisfying than turning your passion into a business. Also, passion can be the differentiating factor between success and failure for any entrepreneur.

The love, drive, and ambition to do what you do, and the ability to see things differently than others—that is passion.

For entrepreneurs, passion is the motivation to serve the world in a way that others can only envision. For example, Jeff Bezos had the vision to create a digital store that sells everything as well as the passion to build it. Steve Jobs had the vision to create a phone with only a single button on the front of the screen as well as the drive to build it.

Richard Branson, the founder of Virgin, said that without passion for your business you will lack the following qualities:

- Drive
- Ambition
- Positive emotional arousal
- Engagement
- Commitment
- Confidence in your vision
- Persuasion skills

The absence of all these salient qualities that are mandatory for running a successful business will eventually result in fewer earnings, which will lead to your failure as an entrepreneur.

Conduct Your Own SWOT Analysis

You can conduct your own SWOT analysis, and the results will help you to identify your strengths and weaknesses, along with your passion.

Personal SWOT Analysis

MY STRENGTHS WHAT AM I GREAT AT?	MY WEAKNESSES HOW CAN I IMPROVE? WHAT DO I NEED TO WORK ON?
OPPORTUNITIES WHO/WHAT CAN HELP ME?	THREATS WHAT IS STANDING IN MY WAY?

S STRENGTHS	
W WEAKNESSES	
O OPPORTUNITIES	
T THREATS	

Professional SWOT Analysis

S STRENGTHS	W WEAKNESSES	O OPPORTUNITIES	T THREATS
• Things your company does well • Where you are better than your competitors • Business resources such as skilled staff • Assets such as intellectual property, innovative technology etc.	• Things your company lacks • Things your competitors do better than you • Areas where your resources are limited • Poor team culture • Lack of unique selling proposition	• New markets for specific products • Few competitors in your area • Emerging trends or needs for your products or services • Press/media coverage of your company	• Emerging competitors • Changing regulatory environment • Negative press/media coverage/reviews • Customers' attitudes changing towards your company

S STRENGTHS

W WEAKNESSES

O OPPORTUNITIES

T THREATS

Passion enables you to capitalise on your drive and ambition to succeed as an entrepreneur. A passionate entrepreneur has the capacity to persevere even when they face obstacles. Furthermore, an entrepreneur with a passion for their business can motivate and persuade clients effectively. This will translate into better income, sales growth and revenues than those businesses run by entrepreneurs who lack passion. A passionate entrepreneur has a better chance of succeeding in business than one who lacks it.

*"Passion. It lies in all of us. Sleeping... waiting...
and though unwanted, unbidden, it will still stir....
It speaks to us... guides us."*
— Joss Whedon

Areas of business I am passionate about:

Other things I am passionate about: ....

....
....
....
....
....
....
....
....
....
....

3. Pain

> *"Sometimes we have to soak ourselves in the tears and fears of the past to water our future gardens."*
> — **Suzy Kassem**

Any normal person will avoid pain at any cost, and emotional pain is often considered to be a form of punishment. The overwhelming feeling at times becomes unbearable. However, experts are of the opinion that emotional pain is necessary for our growth; it makes us emotionally stronger. Emotional pain can leave important messages for us and can often become turning points and leverage us toward success.

Pain can be categorised into two types: physical and emotional. At times, one can lead into the other. For the purpose of understanding the importance of pain in entrepreneurship, we will consider emotional pain. This is a condition where a person is overwhelmed with feelings of sadness, guilt, shame, depression, and fear. When we are exposed to these feeling for a prolonged period of time, they will affect our physical condition and can also translate into physical pain.

At some point in our lives—whether we like it or not—we will face pain that has been caused by failure, loss or separation. It is important to identify the painful situations that you have gone through. Identifying them will help you to process the situation and the messages that they have left for you.

Without identifying the painful incidents in your life, you will fail to:
- Realise the importance of life, family, and friends
- Gain a clear focus and purpose in life
- Make any positive changes to your life
- Create the impetus to achieve something more

Often in entrepreneurship, identifying pain and how to leverage it is important. Painful incidents in your life can be used to gain wisdom, which can then be used as a driving force to do better and be better.

It is not always possible to use pain as a positive force in life. A coach can help you do that. Coaches are equipped to put that pain in perspective and use it as a symbol of courage that grants you the power to do better in life. As an entrepreneur, you will always need courage and determination to succeed. Pain can be used by you to gain the emotional strength required for success.

> *"It may be unfair, but what happens in a few days, sometimes even a single day, can change the course of a whole lifetime."*
> — ***Khaled Hosseini***

Identify your pain here: ....

....

....

....

How can you use this pain to leverage yourself forward?

....

....

....

....

....

Simon Sinek said: *"Champions are not the ones who always win races — champions are the ones who get out there and try. And try harder the next time. And even harder the next time. 'Champion' is a state of mind. They are devoted. They compete to best themselves as much if not more than they compete to best others."*

In his famous speech in Paris, France on 23 April 1910, Theodore Roosevelt pointed to the bravery of those who try and persist.

> *It is not the critic who counts; not the man who points out how the strong man stumbles, or where the doer of deeds could*

have done them better. *The credit belongs to the man who is actually in the arena, whose face is marred by dust and sweat and blood; who strives valiantly; who errs, who comes short again and again, because there is no effort without error and shortcoming; but who does actually strive to do the deeds; who knows great enthusiasms, the great devotions; who spends himself in a worthy cause; who at the best knows in the end the triumph of high achievement, and who at the worst, if he fails, at least fails while daring greatly, so that his place shall never be with those cold and timid souls who neither know victory nor defeat.*

4. People

> *"Stay positive and happy. Work hard and don't give up hope. Be open to criticism and keep learning. Surround yourself with happy, warm and genuine people."*
> **— Tena Desae**

We are social beings. It is impossible for us to survive without the support of other people. Even as an entrepreneur, you will need the support of people to succeed. To become a successful entrepreneur, it is crucial that we surround ourselves with supportive people, who will provide us with positive energy and be champions of our dreams and ventures.

As an entrepreneur, when you have a group of people who share the determination to achieve the same goal that you envision, then by definition you have a team. The success of a business often rests as much on the team as it does on its founder. Selecting a group of people who will support you is important. Richard Branson does this better than most, he builds people and supports them and they support his vision.

"The fundamental driver of our success at Virgin has, and will always be, our people working together," says Richard Branson. "To be successful in business, and in life, you need to connect and collaborate."

Becoming an entrepreneur is a hard decision to make, and the journey to success is tough. If you do not have people on board with you—for example, your immediate family and friends—the journey becomes even harder.

Without a supportive group of people on your road to success, you will fail to:
- Impress investors, because they consider your team when evaluating your project
- Execute your best-laid plans
- Define the culture of your start-up
- Have people who will complement your skills
- Have people who will bring synergy to your efforts
- Have people who will support you when the journey gets tough.

As an entrepreneur, you have to arm yourself with people who can help you and your business grow. Start looking for people who can help you.

> *"When it comes to business success it's all about people, people, people."*
> **— Richard Branson**

As an entrepreneur, identifying people's strengths is important. You are the leader, and, as part of that, you need to know the skills of the people around you. Plan to hire people who can complement you as your business starts to grow. Building the right team with the right people will always prove to be beneficial for you and your business. Richard Branson's top tip for hiring is this: "The first thing to look for when searching for a great employee is somebody with a personality that fits with your company culture."

The cost of a negative employee or business partner is too great a burden on your success and the success of your business. A Harvard Business School[15] study found that "toxic workers" spread negativity and impact your business. Toxic people gossip, are lazy and often feel superior to others.

The study included data on more than 50,000 employees and found that those who carry this "toxic personality" can cause a lot of damage to a company—including the loss of customers, employee morale and even financial loss. The main thing they do is drive other good employees to quit their jobs.

But here's the interesting part of the study—firing your "toxic personality" and reducing the negative behaviour of their toxic culture can result in savings of up to $12,500.

And on the positive side, a positive superstar performer, described as a person "that models desired values and delivers consistent performance" will save a company thousands and will spread positive energy.

---

15. Harvard Business School, 'Toxic Workers'– Housman, Michael Cornerstone OnDemand, Minor, Dylan, Harvard, Kellogg School of Management, Northwestern University, November 2015 Working Paper 16-057.

The people who will help my business are: ....

....
....
....
....
....
....
....
....
....
....

5. Positioning

> *"In a competitive, crowded world market, it's the well positioned brands that stand out!"*
> — ***Bernard Kelvin Clive***

If and when you decide to enter the world of entrepreneurship and marketing, you will hear the term 'positioning' quite a lot. Every company, brand, and entrepreneur tries to position their product. In this day and age, everyone wants a clear and tight position in the market, allowing them to make their claims stick in the minds of prospective customers.

In the world of marketing, 'positioning' refers to how you differentiate your service or product from that of your competitors while deciding which market niche you intend to fill with your product or service.

An entrepreneur needs to position their business in such a way that it can fill a gap in the market.

Every business needs to position their products. However, prior to positioning, an established business goes through a series of sacrosanct steps of segmenting and targeting.

For any new company, the last part—that is, positioning—is crucial because without it an entrepreneur will fail to:
- Identify a gap in the market
- Find a niche in the market
- Find a target audience
- Identify competitors
- Create a Unique Selling Position for your own product.

Positioning your business or product will allow you to know how your business or product will suit the target market's requirements.

With the knowledge of how to position your business, you will know the strengths of your business and eventually how to brand it. By identifying your industry positioning along with your timeline positioning, you will know how to project your product with respect to the needs of the target market. Ultimately, this positioning will help you establish your business's brand identity or image so that consumers will perceive it in a certain way.

> *"Talent is great but being in the right place at the right time is better."*
> *— Endale Edith*

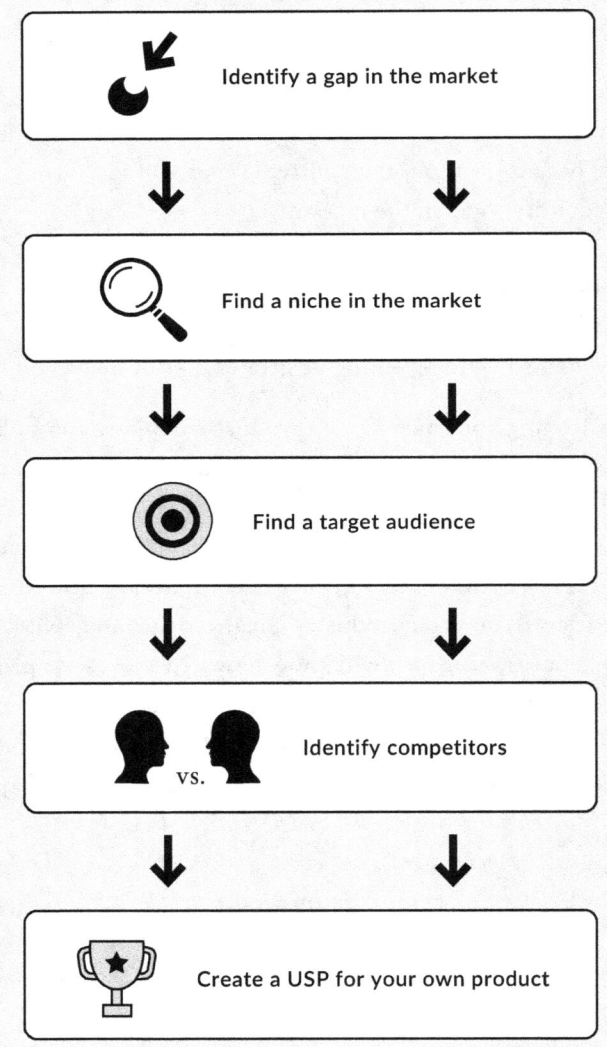

6. Prepare

> *"By failing to prepare, you are preparing to fail."*
> — **Benjamin Franklin**

'Prepare' refers to where you start your business-related actions. You are well prepared when you have done your homework on yourself first by sorting out the strengths and weaknesses of your skills as they relate to your business. Knowing something at a high level is not good enough to lead a business. You need to polish your skills, do deeper research on what else needs to be done. For example, if your business has any connection to recent technology, then you need to be up to date on those technologies and how they have been implemented in similar industries.

Ideas are important for a business. However, preparing yourself with proper skills and resources is more important. Many people have not only good but great ideas. However, they do not develop their skills. Complacency, laziness, contentment arising from the contemplation of the idea without taking the proper follow up action, and so on—these are the common causes that explain why people fail despite their great business ideas.

If you are well prepared with your business skills—that is, if you have polished your inherent skills and have developed the new skills required for your business—then the first thing you will feel is confidence. Even when recruiting people, you will have insight and clarity regarding what kind of person you are looking to hire.

Preparation often involves deeper research, investigation into what you can do to be triumphant in your endeavours.

Abraham Lincoln said, "Give me six hours to chop down a tree and I will spend the first four sharpening the axe."

This is preparation.

How can you sharpen your axe?

Ways I can prepare for success:

---

7. Product

> *When the product is right, you don't*
> *have to be a great marketer.*
> *— Lee Iacocca*

At this stage, you will be focusing on your product (or service). It is a common trend that people jump into marketing their product once they decide to do business. But I suggest you should do extensive research on your product or service.

The following questions can help you:
- What is the demand for your product?
- What are the similar products or services already on the market?
- How is your product or service different from the others?

You may consider the following questions regarding your product, which is the basis of your business. These may appear to be simple but they are very important.

Why your product?
In the majority of cases, business ideas arise out of existing resources and skills. People try to add one or two more dimensions to make their own product better than the existing ones on the market. And then there are people who come up with truly new ideas. The challenge in making both types of product is the same: namely, discovering what makes them unique. If your product is not unique, your business will not survive in a competitive market.

You need to have a thorough knowledge of your own product as well as similar products with high market demand. You must also have a similar knowledge of businesses that have been successful. If you do these things, then you will be able to set a high standard in making your own product unique. You will be able to have informed pricing and presentation strategies, which will allow you to compete with existing competitors in the market.

Remember your product or service must be relevant to the customer not the company.

> *Relevant Positioning:*
> *The positioning must be relevant to the consumer rather than to the company.*

Here's an example of how you can brainstorm the PRICING position of your product.

	HIGH PRICE, LOW QUALITY	HIGH PRICE, HIGH QUALITY
PRICE		
	LOW PRICE, LOW QUALITY	LOW PRICE, HIGH QUALITY

QUALITY

PRODUCT POSITIONING MAP

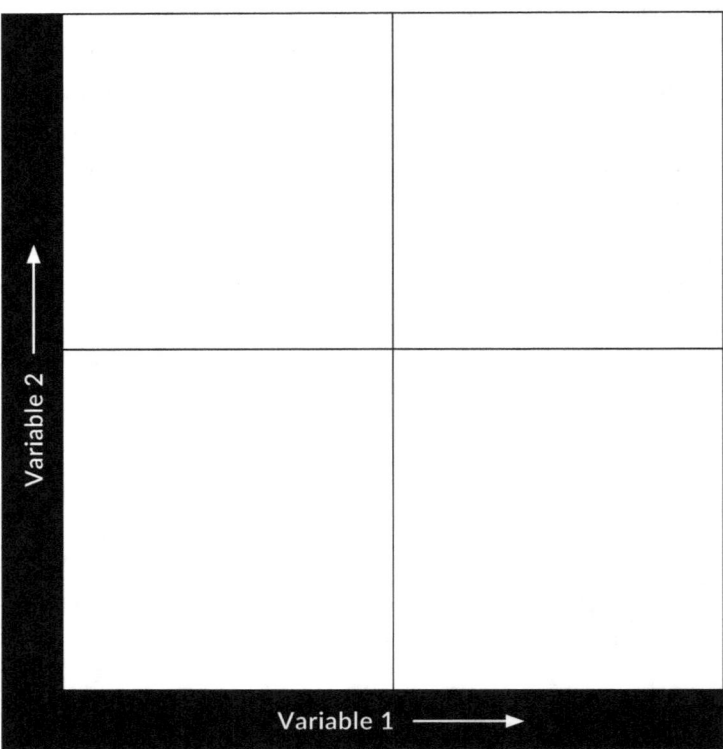

You can fill the variable L-shaped borders in with anything that is important in your industry.

Innovation.

Price.

Customer ease.

8. Promote

> *"If you are on social media, and you are not learning, not laughing, not being inspired or not networking, then you are using it wrong."*
> **— Germany Kent**

'Promote' refers to the make it or break it strategy of your business: How you will design your product or service and how you will be reaching your targeted clients. In a nutshell, your marketing strategy is the key to success for your business.

Until a few years ago, marketing strategies would vary between products and services. However, recent market trends have followed a common path: digital marketing. Digital marketing is available and accessible anywhere, anytime, by anyone and has become the most popular marketing platform.

Becoming a market leader depends on the branding of your product or service. Your branding should be comprehensive. It should make your brand name familiar with a wide range of people, have visual appeal (the look and feel/aesthetics), and open up opportunities for referrals through word of mouth— both real life and virtual—and so on. By doing this, you will create a trust factor regarding your product/business.

Without proper promotional strategies, there will always be a chance that your business/products/services will remain unnoticed among many competitors. Despite having good business ideas/products/strategies, many businesses do not survive in the market or do not achieve their goals due to a lack of marketing strategies.

If you can promote your business/products/services through smart marketing strategies, your business will have a wider client reach. Moreover, through the proper utilisation of online resources, your business can also have a global client reach.

Here are just a few great digital marketing options:

- Content Marketing
- Search Engine Optimisation (SEO)
- Search Engine Marketing (SEM)
- Local Search Marketing
- Remarketing
- Viral Marketing
- Responsive Web Design
- Social Media Marketing (SMM)
- Pay-Per-Click Advertising (PPC)
- Affiliate Marketing
- Email Marketing
- Instant Messaging Marketing
- Marketing Automation
- Influencer Marketing
- Video – YouTube, Vimeo
- Blogs
- Google Adwords
- Google
- Plus More...

Jobs you can create and have in digital marketing:

- Email Marketer
- Affiliate Marketer
- Search Engine Specialist
- Online Advertising Specialist
- Social Media Marketer
- Online Reputation Manager
- Digital Account Manager
- Digital Campaign Manager
- Advert Specialist
- AdWords Specialist
- Online Entrepreneur
- Marketplace Manager
- Web content Manager
- Online Leads Manager
- Ecommerce Specialist
- Web Analytics Executive
- SEO Specialist
- Viral Marketer
- Content creation Manager
- Blogger
- Vlogger
- Influencer
- Analytics Manager
- CRM and Email marketing Manager
- Digital Sales Director
- Copywriter
- Digital Marketing Manager and Web Manager
- Ecommerce Manager
- PPC Search Manager
- Search Manager / SEO Manager.
- Product Marketing Specialist

Social Media Marketing

Over the years, there has been a significant rise in social media. There are currently around 3.4 billion social media users globally, and research shows that it is more effective, accurate, and has far better ROI than traditional media and advertising.

Companies and organisations have recognised it; hence, they have leveraged the advantage of digital marketing strategy to grow their business.

For this purpose, companies are looking for professionals trained in social media marketing. As a result, the demand for people certified in social media marketing and training is on the rise. So if you enrol yourself in social media marketing training the chances of achieving your goals and reaping the benefits of the digital marketing world will be enormous. Some of the benefits of getting trained in social media marketing are:

Find the Professional In You
Social media marketing is the most growing and booming industry. So if you want to get the skill set that is demanded by the companies who will be hiring or have already started to utilise the professionals with social media marketing experience, enrol yourself in a social media marketing training courses. You will get the required skills and expertise to secure the job and become a professional.

Broaden Your Career Choices
Many organisations are now offering different digital marketing and social media marketing jobs and career profiles. Even enterprises like Twitter, Facebook, Google, etc., are offering a wide variety of jobs in social media marketing. If you have the required skill sets that you can easily get by enrolling in a social media marketing training, you can be choosy to apply for jobs that align with your expertise.

Higher Salary
One of the alluring aspects of social media marketing training course is that on completion, you get a job, with a higher salary than those without the training. A certificate in social media marketing will ensure that you have better skills in managing and marketing any product on social media sites and other

digital platforms. If you have the experience and the certificate, then you are in the position to negotiate your salary for a better package than those without the training.

Start Your Career
With social media marketing training, you can start your career with a basic qualification. Unlike most professional, certificate and diploma courses in for undergraduate level, the pre-requisites are quite a lot. However, with social media marketing courses, you can start your career anytime and work without leaving your home. There are several courses and tests that you can apply to become a qualified social media marketing professional and start your career.

Enjoy The Flexibility
The flexibility to work from home and at any time in social media marketing is quite an added advantage for people who face problems leaving home for work. All you need is an internet connection, and an online social media marketing training course to show you the ropes of the trade. Once you have the skills, you can start the work as a freelancer or start your own business and enjoy the benefits of the training.

Deployment of Skills
With social media marketing skills being used by all business types, be it small, medium or large, you can easily use your skills from one company to the other. Mainly if you are a freelancer as a social media marketing professional, you can use the knowledge that you have learned at the social media marketing training at any of the works you do in social media marketing for any company. All you need is to be a bit creative.

Show Your Creativity

The aim of social media marketing is to create the buzz, and hype about a product, dormant blog, service, and website. To do that you require creativity and logic. The ability to write concise content in a few words, make a strategy and creative that will grab the attention of the audience is vital. Social media marketing training will train you to think outside the box.

9. Profit

> *"The promise of every product and service is a better life.*
> *Profits are the prize for delivering on the promise."*
> **— Patrick Dixon**

Profit is the money a business pulls in after accounting for all expenses.

Profit is something this program is designed to get you.

Tony Robbins has a plan listed on his website about how to achieve profit and as you will see, my program includes some of these strategies too.

These are his top ways to make and increase profit. He suggests to:

» **Think in terms of small steps**

Create a business map that helps you think in terms of incremental growth and a steady plan to increase profit. Plan for today, this week, this month and this year. He suggests to work with a business coach and make your profit plan scalable.

» **Identify what is holding you back**
Tony suggests to take an objective look at your business and see what is preventing you from making the money you know you're capable of earning? What personal or professional tools do you need to breakthrough?

» **Find where you can drive growth**
Look at your product, people and find opportunities where you can drive maximum growth.

» **Add real value to your customers**
Find ways to fill the need of your customer and add real and massive value.

» **Focus on strategic innovation**
Identify who your customer really is and why they need your unique product or service. How can you be strategic in your business and innovation?

» **Supercharge your connections**
Think about your network, strategic alliances, partnerships and people. How can you maximise these awesome connections?

» **Customise your engagement**
Use personal and customer-focused engagement tools and marketing for your clients.

» **Make a plan of action**
Create massive action plans and goals to generate growth.

» **Track your progress**
Monitor what is working and what isn't—monitor and plan your progress.

"If you're passionate about something and you work hard, then I think you will be successful."
— **Pierre Omidyar, eBay Founder and Chairman**

THE PROGRAM TO PROFIT

If you want to quit your job and become a digital entrepreneur all you need to do is follow the above **9P Business Strategy**.

My program will be the best 180 days of your business life. You will never look back!

Still not convinced? Let me show you more.

The program includes:
- Online Business workshop. I will teach you how to utilise the 9P Business Strategy to quit your job and develop a solid digital business. You will also learn presentation, sales and leadership skills during this journey.
- Idea generations. I will sit with you and validate ideas to ensure you can come up with an idea to generate income for you.
- Product Design. We will develop a digital product so you can be ready for the market.
- Social Media marketing. I will teach you how you can

utilise the power of social media and bring leads in the business.
- Funnel set up. I will also teach you how you can set up an integrated funnel to run your business.
- Business Automations. Automation is an integrated part of the business so you can focus more on business development and give time to family or precious people in your life.
- Face-to-face email and phone support as well as special access to a private Facebook group where new content is uploaded regularly. This content is timeless and crucial for anyone in business to stay up-to-date with the latest trends.
- Access to support from other entrepreneurs and opportunities to engage with other like-minded people.
- Help with marketing, website building, social media, and getting leads.

Still not convinced? You will also get me as your **Mentor for 1 year** so I can help you to follow my proven steps to become a Digital Entrepreneur.

YOU WILL be given proven steps to creating, growing and transitioning into **A Digital Entrepreneur in 180 days**.

"You will never go broke from investing in yourself."
— Hemi Hossain

Purpose

Our purpose in Grow With Hemi is to provide a platform to individuals who wish to learn more or further their career in Digital Marketing or become an Entrepreneur. We not only help you to make money but succeed in your life with the right motivation.

Change the way business is done! Through Hemi's signature program, your dream of being an ENTREPRENEUR will become a reality. Learn these essential skills and mindsets that every entrepreneur should know.

Grow With Hemi is a platform that offers more than just courses in Digital Marketing and Entrepreneurship. We help you to establish connections with the community of professionals who are in the same field. As part of the ever-growing community of Grow With Hemi, you can access the latest education and technology that you would require to achieve your goals.

> *"Formal education will make you a living;*
> *self-education will make you a fortune."*
> *— Jim Rohn*

We have also following services are available under our brand.

DIGITAL EXPLORATION PROGRAM

Utilise your coaching or consulting skills, move to online and explode your sales in the next 90 days.

What is the program:

The program has been designed for Coaches and Consultants who are ready to move online and utilise the power of social media and accelerate their business.

This program has designed to teach you how to run a coaching and consulting business online during in this pandemic. This is not only teaching, my expert team will do the work for you so that you can continue after finishing the training.

We will teach you:
- The Fastest Way To Learn The Power of Online Entrepreneurship So You Can Move Your Business Online in 90 days.
- Our Expert Team Will Do The All Work For You.

BUSINESS MENTORING AND COACHING PROGRAM

Are you struggling with your business and not sure what to do and how to progress?

This is a very customised program for you. I will assess your individual needs and come up with a 1-year plan to take your business to the next level.

I will also develop a digital strategy roadmap for your business to grow.

I am in here to support you and will develop your team as well so that they can align with your vision.

I Will Teach You The Fastest Way to Grow Your Business And Become a Digital Entrepreneur

Community

You get connected to like-minded people and community of entrepreneurs who share their priceless advice with you online, in-person and in group discussions.

> *"I knew that if I failed I wouldn't regret that, but I knew the one thing I might regret is not trying."*
> — *Jeff Bezos, Amazon Founder and CEO*

ABOUT HEMI

Hemi Hossain is a self-made success story whose mission is to help others grow and develop so they can be more successful and happy. He is the man who has built an entire domain as a Business Coach and Digital Entrepreneur.

Hemi is an international speaker, author, investor and winner of Best Business Award in Melbourne, 2018 and featured in many national and international media around the globe. He also won Young Entrepreneur of the Year In Bangladesh in 2017.

The journey to becoming a successful entrepreneur and coach was tough for Hemi since the decision to leave the comfortable life of an executive originated from a couple of painful personal events. However, he turned his situation around and saw them as stepping stones to success.

Hemi is a certified Human Behaviour Consultant and Hypnosis coach and Neuro-Linguistics Programming (NLP) practitioner. His work as an entrepreneur and philanthropist has received both national and international coverage in print and television media.

Hemi is the Managing Director of a successful digital marketing company with a strong interest in advertising, media, tech and different projects all around the globe.

Hemi has inspired the lives of over 1 million people in 4 different countries, from over 100 industries on and offline through his mentoring and coaching. Hemi Hossain believes in cumulative success and gauges his own achievement by seeing the success of the people he coaches.

Hemi is sharing more in his INTERACTIVE book.

See exclusive, behind-the-scenes videos, audios and photos.

DOWNLOAD free content and learn how to Grow With Hemi.

growwithhemi.com/interactive

TESTIMONIALS

Thank you Hemi for everything. You have changed my life. I always wanted to become a coach and trainer. I am so fortunate, I have met you and now I am progressing towards that path. The thing about Hemi that attracted me is focusing on values and discipline on the top of everything. To me, he is more specific and accurate and on point to the need. My purpose was to join his session to know and find myself. I have lost myself. I am believing that I choose the right one.

Iftekhar Iftee

People should be driven by their mission and vision, but very few of us are actually able to find that mission and vision of life. Thanks to the Grow With Hemi Program and the Diploma In Digital Entrepreneurship Program, I have found mine. Now I am a successful life coach in Bangladesh.

Without Hemi, it would not have been possible, he shaped me in a way where I can continue my journey. I wish him very best of luck with his amazing program. Grow With Hemi!

GM Iftekher Ifti
Founder Biohacker at Mindvana Academy

I am a fashion designer and entrepreneur. I started my career by working for some famous fashion boutique houses. I started feeling that I was not doing what I always wanted. I wanted to start my own fashion house but I wasn't confident. Then I found Hemi and his Diploma In Digital Entrepreneurship Program. I attended some of his sessions and engaged in a 1-on-1 with him. His two-day bootcamp was a game-changer. I found the courage and confidence to start my own boutique house. It was a massive success and now I am the owner of "Kahon Fashion Studio". I would like to thank Mr. Hemi. I am very lucky that I found a great mentor like him

Sharmin Mustika Mili
Fashion Designer & Owner of Kahon Fashion Studio

I am a health coach, I work with executives and corporate owners. Previously, I charged by the hour and by the client, which was a massive burden for further growth. Through Hemi's Diploma In Digital Entrepreneurship program, I have learned these necessary skills and Hemi also provided me with a personalized and customized solution. Thank you, Hemi, I wish you a very best of luck in your journey of creating 1000 entrepreneurs by 2020.

Tanya
Health Coach

Today I was invited by Hemi, from Grow with Hemi, to talk at a summit he ran on 'Employee to Entrepreneur.' I always saw the potential in Hemi throughout his career in Telstra & I've loved watching him build multiple businesses. I was his Boss and now learning from Hemi. Hemi is such great Coach and Mentor.

Brooke Earle

What's everyone doing on their Saturday morning. I don't want to be the 90% that aren't doing anything. It's raining and cold but I've jumped out of bed and went to learn more from my mentor and coach. Today he has taken me to the next level!! Hemi Hossain, you are a great coach and mentor.

Mana Sands

I am so happy to be part of Hemi's Inner Circle!! I have attended his seminar and joined his program. I followed his teachings to the point and I have to tell you it is not for everyone in the beginning even I was thinking that this is an impossible journey but I figured if Hemi Hossain can succeed then definitely I should build up the courage to fire my own boss too. First time entrepreneurs face many challenges, but I believe Hemi Hossain's wisdom will at least give the winning mindset to take the right decisions and take massive immediate action.

Ismail Syed

IF YOU TAKE MY PROGRAM, I PERSONALLY GUARANTEE THAT YOU WILL...

- » Gain More Business Knowledge
- » Discover New Working Opportunities
- » Find New Success
- » Gain New Confidence
- » Develop New Business Tools and Skills
- » Live Smarter and Better
- » Learn How to Have More Time, Money and Freedom

Hemi Hossain
www.growwithhemi.com

END NOTES

1. *Journal of Personality*, 2014, Yes, but are they happy? Effects of trait self-control on affective well-being and life satisfaction. Hofmann W(1), Luhmann M, Fisher RR, Vohs KD, Baumeister RF. University of Chicago.. Epub 2013 Aug 8.

2. Dweck, C.S.; Legget, E.L. (1988). "A social-cognitive approach to motivation and personality". *Psychological Review.* 95 (2): 256–273. doi:10.1037/0033-295x.95.2.256.

3. Lipton PhD, Bruce. "How to Maintain the Infamous Honeymoon-Period-of-Bliss." Published blog online October 25, 2018. www.brucelipton.com/blog/how-maintain-the-infamous-honeymoon-period-bliss

4. Randler, Christoph. (2009). Proactive People Are Morning People1. Journal of Applied Social Psychology. 39. 2787-2797. 10.1111/j.1559-1816.2009.00549.x.

5. Randler, Christoph, Defend Your Research: The Early Bird Really Does Get the Worm, *Harvard Business Review*, 2010, online article.

6. Utton, Dominic, Boost your mood with music: what to play throughout the day, *The Telegraph*, Feb 6, published online 2018.

7. Gail Matthews, Professor, *Goals Research Summary*, Dominican University of California, 2015.

8. Charron S, Koechlin E. Divided representation of concurrent goals in the human frontal lobes. Science. 328(360), 360-363 (2010).

Clapp W, Rubens M, Sabharwal J, Gazzaley A. Deficit in switching between functions underlies the impact of multitasking memory in older adults. Proceedings of the National Academy of Sciences of the United States of America. 108(17), 7212-7217 (2011).

9. McKay; Brett; Kate (October 23, 2013). "The Eisenhower Decision Matrix: How to Distinguish Between Urgent and Important Tasks and Make Real Progress in Your Life". *A Man's Life, Personal Development.*

10. Mark, Gloria, Gudith, Daniela, Klocke, Ulrich, 2008/01/01, The cost of interrupted work: More speed and stress – 10.1145/1357054.1357072. Conference on Human Factors in Computing Systems – Proceedings

11. Yoerger, Michael; Crowe, John; and Allen, Joseph A., "Participate or Else!: The Effect of Participation in Decision-Making in Meetings on Employee Engagement" (2015). Psychology Faculty Publications. 120. https://digitalcommons.unomaha.edu/psychfacpub/120

12. Young Entrepreneur Council (YEC), https://yec.co

13. Gartner, Gartner Top Strategic Predictions for 2020 and Beyond, published online October 22, 2019.

14. Salesforce Research, *2016 State of Marketing Report*: Trends and insights from nearly 4,000 marketing leaders worldwide.

15. Harvard Business School, 'Toxic Workers'– Housman, Michael Cornerstone OnDemand, Minor, Dylan, Harvard, Kellogg School of Management, Northwestern University, November 2015 Working Paper 16-057.

BOOK REFERENCES

Corley, Thomas. *Rich Habits: The Daily Success Habits of Wealthy Individuals.* 2009. Langdon Street Press. Minneapolis, USA

Covey, Stephen R. *The 7 Habits Of Highly Effective People: Restoring The Character Ethic.* New York Free Press, 2004. Print.

Kiyosaki, Robert T, and Sharon L. Lechter. *Rich Dad, Poor Dad: What the Rich Teach Their Kids About Money That the Poor and Middle Class Do Not!* Paradise Valley, Ariz: TechPress, 1998

Lipton PhD, Bruce. *The Biology of Belief,* Hay House, October 2015.

www.ingramcontent.com/pod-product-compliance
Lightning Source LLC
Chambersburg PA
CBHW071453080526
44587CB00014B/2087